AF253391

The Woman Who Walks The Earth

(Ki Wahine Ko Hikoi Te Whenua)

LEIGH ROSS

The Journey Begins…

Copyright © 2015 Leigh Ross
All rights reserved.
ISBN: 978-0-473-32465-0

DEDICATION

I dedicate this book to all those who have suffered. To all those who have lost their way at some point or have felt they have lost all purpose, this is for you. Know that regardless of the situation, you are supported by your loving guides and helpers and there is a greater purpose in it all. We are all connected through our Divine Consciousness so your pain is mine and your Joy is mine also – we are all in this journey together.
It is my hope that my story may help someone in some small way on their journey, as we all struggle to put the pieces together.

And to Titus – a Warrior of the Light

CONTENTS

ACKNOWLEDGMENTS

For all who have supported and accepted me –
I know it wasn't easy at times but I have every bit of faith that it
was for a higher purpose, and you are blessed for the role you
chose to take in my life. *Thank you*

DISCLAIMER

While this is a *true story*, the names of those involved have been
changed to protect their privacy

1 WHEN IT RAINS IT POURS

It was raining again, for the third cool spring day.

As I looked out of my office window I wondered if it would ever end. Just one sunny day would give me reason to take some time off; something that was drastically missing in my life.

My thoughts were shattered as the loud obnoxious ringtone of the phone screamed out to be answered.

"Hello, East Coast Bays Centre" I said.

The familiar voice on the other end seemed agitated and somewhat confused.

"Hi Leigh, its Terry. I think we have a problem this weekend."

"Oh" I said with almost no shock factor.

"Yes, it seems that the cricket club has organised a function for Saturday night - the same night our prize-giving is on!"

I could hear panic in his voice but it sounded more like a whingeing child

"Hold on" I said, "Let me grab my function book and check it out... Well, they're booked in for the following weekend so someone's got his dates mixed up. It's not my writing so I'll find out who's it is. I'll give Peter a call and get right back with you. Are you at work?"

"Yeah, I'll be here 'till around three" Terry's voice reflected a sense of relief in that yet again I would 'sort it out'.

The problem I had from day one in this job was getting all the different committees to work together. For some reason the committees despised each other and I was often left as the middle man at the last minute needing to rearrange a couple of thousand people.

I tracked Peter down at home and when he heard the problem he became irate, yelling at me and accusing me of not doing my job properly. He then began accusing Terry of sabotaging his function.

I noticed how I had tuned out. His voice was now a distant murmur in the background. My eyes were fixed on the rain splashing against the shiny two-year-old aluminium window ledge.

The room sounded eerily quiet and my senses felt numb, as if caught in a never-ending spiralling tunnel, or a state of suspended time.

I began to feel a strange sensation in my chest. At first it felt like heartburn but quickly turned in to an unfamiliar pain I can only relate to someone reaching in through my ribs, taking hold of my heart and squeezing it tightly as they twisted it inside me.

Everything became still again and as I tried to open my eyes I realised they already were, yet everything around me was concealed with a soft and somewhat familiar white haze.

I had no idea how long I had been hunched over in my chair but as I moved my head my vision cleared to a faint blur and I noticed the rain had stopped.

The pain in my chest had subsided but my arms and legs remained numb.

The phone was still resting in my hand and I could hear the faint beeping on the line to let me know the call had ended although I had no recollection of finishing the conversation.

I gathered myself together and managed to organise a drink of water as my mouth felt like a scouring pad.

I made a cup of tea then sat down to try to take stock of what had just happened.

I re-ran it all through my mind, moment by moment, again and again, coming to the conclusion I must have fainted. But why? Was it lack of sleep? No, it can't have been. Last night was one of the best nights rest I'd had in a while. I hadn't been out clubbing in a few nights so it wasn't from partying too hard. I had eaten a good breakfast… I couldn't understand it.

The pain in my chest kept bringing me back to a deep inner knowing that stress was the cause. Somehow I overloaded and my system just couldn't take any more.

The thought scared me but the more I thought about it the more I knew I had just experienced something like a stroke or heart attack. I wasn't sure what to do about it – do I go to the hospital? I feel ok right now so maybe I was overreacting.

The feeling had almost come back to my fingers so I reached for the yellow pages and decided I would at least call and ask.

I thumbed through the 'H's' in the hefty directory looking for the local hospital listing when an ad jumped out at me. It was under the 'Hypnotists' section and the part that jumped out was the name 'Christophe Christianson'.

I thought it was a strange name but something resonated within me and I felt drawn to the 'Christ' part of his names.

I had always believed in Christ, in my own way. I had never felt comfortable with what had been taught to me in church but in this moment it seemed like a signpost hitting me on the head to take notice.

My fingers seemed to dial the number automatically and before I knew it I had an appointment set up for the following morning.

What a day already, and it wasn't even lunchtime!

The sound of heavy work boots on the polished wooden floor echoed off the newly painted walls and blended to create a unique rhythm with the unmistakable pitter-patter of Larry's adorable boxer companion.

Beaming as always, Larry poked his head around the door while Lucy wriggled her way past him to jump up and greet me with her whole body twisting to and fro; the excitement and energy synonymous with a boxer.

My day instantly brightened every time I saw her.

"How's it going?" Larry asked in his usual laid-back manner.

"Oh, its fine I guess. I've had quite a weird morning though. Oh, while you're here, do you know anything about this booking next weekend?" I reached for the function book and pointed out the dates in question.

"Yeah" He said. "I took that booking last week. Peter organised it. He wrote it in there."

"Oh" I replied. "He's claiming that his function is this weekend" Larry quickly responded

"No, no, no. He was careful about writing it in there and anyway he said he was going to need a couple of weeks to organise it." He was shaking his head with frustration.

"Ok then, I'll let him know, thanks Larry."

I was glad that was cleared up. I was not getting paid enough to get in between these bickering battles. I knew that the Trust Board, whom I was employed by, weren't really paying me what the job was worth. I was getting just over half what the previous Manager was.

My age and gender had held me back on a number of occasions. I was young, I knew it, but I had worked really hard to be where I was.

I had started my hospitality career in the bar. Despite only being seventeen the assistant manager had seen my enthusiasm, hired me and I learnt quickly.

I became a well-respected bartender, not only by fellow workers but management as well.

I however had my heart set on becoming a manager and would often tell the Hotel General Manager of this aspiration.

He did what he could for me, putting my name forward to the Breweries for their training scheme but they always turned me down. "You're too young. We feel nervous about spending $70,000 on training you when you're more than likely going to get married and pregnant; wasting our investment."

I, however, didn't let that stop me. I had no desire to get married, and having children was nowhere in my grand scheme of things, so after-hours I worked alongside the Bar Manager, helping him out while gradually learning everything I could about his job.

Several years later when that Bar Manager was given a better opportunity, I applied for his position.

The Bar Manager had written out a reference for me and had detailed all the extra work I had done in my own time, which shocked the General Manager who gave me the job without hesitation.

That job had carried me through a few years and provided the ultimate social life environment, enabling me to drink away all my problems. I didn't once have to think about my life, I could just drink it into oblivion. It didn't cost me anything and it was quite normal for me to be either still drunk the next day or at the very least, hung over.

I didn't even realise I had problems until I was sober and felt how unhappy I was. With no support around me, my only available cure was to have another drink.

I guess things about my life had begun to push me to question, but at that time I was scared of the answers or just really didn't know what to do with all these new, strange feelings developing.

I would quite often plummet into deep despair.

I knew I needed Love in my life but I couldn't seem to find it. I continued to try, although not in the best of places.

I was involved with a married man and I liked it that way.

Neither of us had to commit and all we had was a fun, exciting relationship. We would meet three to four times a week at the same club. We would dance, drink, have sex and that was it.

No deep meaningful conversations, no delving into those private spaces I didn't want to share with anyone. It was perfect.

"Do you want a cuppa?" Larry shouted from the kitchen. I looked around the office; surprised I hadn't noticed him leave.

"Sure" I called back as I made my way through the empty hall. "Looked like you were miles away," he said, hinting for me to fill him in.

"I was actually. Things have become pretty weird for me lately. I'm really starting to question my life and what I'm doing with it. You know I set a goal for myself when I was eighteen. I had been working in a bar for a year and decided that I wanted to run my own place by the time I turned twenty-four. Well, here I am. Twenty four last December and I am the General Manager of this impressive club."

Larry looked surprised "You're only twenty four? Now that's something to be proud of."

"Is it really?" I said. "I deal with drunken people every day, in fact, I encourage them to drink. I have to deal with four different committees who all think they know best and who plainly haven't outgrown adolescence. On top of that, the Board; who I'm responsible to, expect me to break Liquor Licensing laws that have two-year prison sentences. They just tell me "not to worry because we have mates that are cops""

Larry was half nodding his head as he handed me my cup.

"You know I've seen a lot of Managers through here in my time. It seems the stress of it gets to all of them at some point".

"Do you know anything about hypnosis?" I asked him.

"No, not really, other than what you see on TV where people make total fools of themselves. Why?"

"I'm going to see one tomorrow. He does a different type of hypnosis, supposed to help relieve stress." I told him.
I could tell he wasn't sure about it but humoured me by asking me to let him know how it goes.

The rest of the day went by slowly. I didn't feel much like working and the following hours seemed like a blur.

I felt a strange loss of drive with absolutely no ambition to do any of the pending tasks.

As the rain began tapping against the window again I questioned, "What am I doing here?" I started to get a sense of something very different happening to me when those thoughts suddenly clamped up and appeared to shoot through a vortex, bringing me back to the moment, sitting in my chair.

Again the phone had interrupted a moment that I felt had the potential to turn my life around.

"Hi Leigh, its Terry again. Do you have any news on Saturday?"

"Yes" I said trying to sound excited for him. "I just spoke with Peter and he swore he'll have my job on a plate but Saturday is all yours."

"Thanks so much" he said, sounding clearly relieved "I'll have a word with some of the Board members and get Peter sorted out. Thanks again Leigh and I'll see you Saturday."

The conversation was still ringing in my ears as I realised I didn't care in the slightest about my job. Yesterday I would have gone out of my way to make everyone happy. Today I simply didn't care.

I gathered up a few papers, putting them in my car before heading to the back of the building where I had a run set up for Jabez, my Belgium shepherd.

I loved having animals around, especially dogs.

I had fond memories of a childhood dog called Troy. He was a German Shepherd that loved to walk all over my clean white clothes with muddy paws when I was a very small baby - or that's the story my Mother told.

I was devastated years later when a man and his son came and took him away. I was told he had become too difficult to handle by always jumping into the front of the car while my mother was trying to drive.

At the time I didn't understand and was heart-broken.

Then along came Brodie, a pedigree boarder collie. She was a lovely dog. Unfortunately she had been left with the man my mother lived with after separating from my father.

Years later after I had left home I got a German Shepherd and named him Troy 2. He was an incredible dog; one that really opened my eyes and understanding of animals.

He mysteriously disappeared while left with my older brother to look after.

We had a cat throughout my childhood, Destry. Again my life was shattered the day I discovered I had been sent away to a friend's place overnight so he could be put down.

I guess my parents thought they were being considerate, but it broke my heart that they had deceived me in that way.

I knew he was old and not in too good health but I had no idea that was coming.

Now my animal companion is a cat called Cling-on. He is a blue Burmese and absolutely hilarious. I got him as a kitten and recently had another cat turn up on the doorstep.

Dad called her 'Annie' after the orphan.
Cling-on and Annie get along really well and spend many hours playing until one of them has had enough and it inevitably turns into a fight, of which Cling-on always wins.

Cling-on had no fear when it comes to dogs and so far has managed to be civil to Jabez who is still very much a puppy.

My animals have been an incredible support to me over the years. Whenever I felt things getting tough, just being around them would lift my spirits.

One of the houses I grew up in had a creek running through the back yard and we kept a large woodpile next to it.

This woodpile would attract wild cats and the feline family living in there would multiply rapidly. I would spend a lot of time sitting next to the woodpile trying to coax the kittens out.

They would very rarely come close enough for me to pick them up but every once in a while I was able to catch them. They would scratch and tear at my arms but that was just a risk I was willing to take.

I wanted to help them by giving them a home so I would put them in a box and call the S.P.C.A. who would care for them until they were adopted.

Now, of course, I realise that the likelihood of these ferocious kittens being adopted was slim and euthanization was probably more in line with what really happened.

My thoughts came back to Jabez as he excitedly jumped into the car. I felt nauseous as I thought of the cruelty we humans inflict upon animals through ignorance.

I headed home still feeling despondent and confused about my life.

I was apprehensive as I pulled into Christopher's driveway the following day. I didn't know what to expect from hypnosis and it wasn't usual for me to be seeking help in the first place.

I was meant to be strong, not showing any weaknesses, and especially not to strangers.

In front of me stood a beautiful old house, surrounded by full and healthy oak trees that appeared to be hugging the recently painted weatherboards.

I was about ten minutes early, which was normal for me. I liked to allow up to half an hour for traffic or in this case finding an area I was unfamiliar with.

I had never ventured into this part of town before but it looked like a nice suburb; clean and tidy with large houses surrounded by immaculate gardens; obviously a wealthy area.

As I stepped out of the car a black cat came trotting up to me. The bell around its neck rang with a tone that was just loud enough to warn any bird-life of his presence but delicate enough to think you were hearing the sound of angels.

Living on an Island such as New Zealand is a blessing with no poisonous insects or reptiles, and no predatory animals that endanger human lives. Unfortunately, out of ignorance and lack of forethought, many animals have been brought in.

Introduced for various reasons they have resulted in the demise and threat of extinction of many native birds and wildlife.

As I patted this beautiful, loving, purring animal I thought of what a huge threat they had become to our beloved 'Kiwi' bird.

I silently thanked the owner of this cat for at least being conscious enough to give birds fair warning of its arrival.

My heart lifted instantly when the cat looked at me and with that all-too-familiar meow, informed me of his need for some attention. Such simplicity and honesty was inspiring.

Together we made our way to the front door. The cat was still entangled between my ankles when Christophe greeted me.

Towering in the doorway, Christophe was an incredibly striking man. Easily over six feet tall, he was bald with a face that reminded me of something out of a King Arthur's story.
His presence was strong and compelling, which encouraged my trust in him.

The cat shot through my legs and disappeared into a room towards the front of the house that I could only imagine had to be the kitchen while Christophe led me down two sets of stairs through long dark hallways.

The walls were covered with pictures of people that looked like saints and angels. The smell of incense wafting through the house reminded me of Hare Krishna gatherings next door to where I grew up.

We came to a small area that served as his treatment room. It was furnished with a simple bed, desk and chair. A large window next to the bed revealed a glorious garden leading down towards a stream.

Everything sparkled with a vibrant, lush radiance after the previous day's rain.

Christophe began by explaining a little about what he does, to give me an idea of the process I would be experiencing.

He warned me that we might not get to do much in the way of hypnosis today as the first visit is more or less an introduction.

Call it Sagittarius' nature, but I told him that I couldn't afford to pay him sixty dollars to just sit and chat, and that I wanted to get as much out of this as I could.

I could see he was a little shocked by my bluntness but he asked what I was there for.

I explained yesterday's experience to him and watched as a smile appeared on his face. It was hidden under a huge moustache that curled up at the sides, but the corresponding glint in his eyes gave it away.

"Yes, hypnosis can help with stress. Hypnosis is a form of meditation. What we're doing is relaxing the body totally. We keep the mind alert and we bring the conscious mind and the sub-conscious mind together. During this process you are totally aware of what's going on – contrary to how hypnosis is perceived in the public eye. I don't do anything like that although the mind is very receptive to suggestion so I could tell you at the end of a session that you won't remember any of it and you wouldn't. So with hypnosis we can 'reprogram' your mind, for simplicity's sake".

Christophe waited for some sign that I understood all he was saying.

"Ok" I said eager to hear more.

He continued, "So, we can go to the source of the 'problem' or the 'stress' by going back to the actual time the event happened. We call this 'regression.' This can take you into past lives as well, as many issues are brought through with us from life to life".

Wow, this was not what I was expecting. It was familiar to me in some way though. Past lives! I had always felt a fascination for past lives and knew they existed in some way.
I would sometimes experience feelings as though I was someone else, a whole other personality and knew at the same time that it was still a part of me somehow. Now I had something tangible to put it all together. I was really excited to get started. I wanted to

find out as much as I could about my past, as there were many holes in my memory, even from this lifetime.

Christophe explained that we'd try to do a relaxation session to check how receptive I would be and explained how some people won't allow themselves to be hypnotised.

I laid down and he placed a blanket over me while explaining how the body temperature quite often drops in a deep state of relaxation. I felt comfortable and excited.

My stomach had butterflies in anticipation.

I closed my eyes and as instructed took several deep breaths.

My head was swirling with thoughts of what was about to happen, along with the many mundane intrusions about things that had happened last week and earlier in the day.

Christophe then led me on a mind journey throughout my body, relaxing every muscle as I focused on it. As we made our way to my head his voice became fuller and seemed to thunder the commands. It was resonating in my head in an almost 'ethereal' way.

I could feel my body responding instantly. As the muscles around my face were relaxed I almost felt like a different person.

Once we reached the top of the head he said he would let me experience the sensations for a few minutes before we moved on.

I lay there with my mind thinking, "This can't be it, I don't feel hypnotised. I feel great, but not hypnotised."

I then felt a strange sensation. It was as though someone had hold of my feet with someone else holding my head and both pulling their respective end, stretching my body! It felt fantastic. I wanted to open my eyes and look but my eyelids were too heavy, so I just surrendered to it.

I had had so many back problems over the years from accidents that this was the first real relief I had felt.

My whole body jolted as the 'thundering' voice caused shock waves to run through it as if hit by lightning.

The words were commanding "I now want you to go back in time to a happy moment of you life. Just relax and let your self go back to this time."

I was instantly aware of my mind racing, heart pounding and strange lights moving around in my head. I felt a wave of energy kick in. I could feel it fire up like a big old engine that hadn't been run in years. Slowly the cogs began turning, faster and faster until it got to just the right pace.

Once it reached the correct velocity my eyes began to flicker, which reminded me of a tape player on rewind.
I could feel myself being drawn or sucked into this 'void' ~ back through time and space. I was flying now, speeding through lights and images of my lifetime, back through my birth, back to where I had come from.

"Where are you?" The voice roared again.

I looked around with my new eyes and all I could see was white light. "I'm waiting in the light" I struggled to say.

My mouth was dry and moving my lips was an extreme effort as they felt heavy and uncomfortable.

"What are you waiting for?" Christophe sounded a little confused.

Again I struggled to move my lips and my jaw which felt like lead, "I'm waiting to be born"

I sensed a shocked reaction from him and there was silence for what seemed like an eternity.

I became aware of feeling his mind; being one with his soul. He was unprepared for what had happened and was struggling to find the next step.

I was in a strange place, in between worlds.

Here I was in another time and place yet I was aware of lying on the bed in this room also. I realised why I had come to earth and was aware that I was aware of everything. As an observer, and reviewing my life in that split second, I thought how sad it was that I had not really felt any real happiness.

The voice commanded again "Come forward now to a time in your present life when you felt the happiest".

Instantly I felt myself being sucked forward, this time at a much slower and more comfortable pace.

I rested at a point where I was aware of a birthday party going on… Oh, it was mine. I was playing with my dog.

I described the scene to Christophe and he encouraged me to move on to another happy time. Again it was like being swept up in a tornado as I went racing back into the blissful, joyous 'white light'.

On hearing this, Christophe commanded me to come back to my body lying on the bed. He began telling me to relax and we would do something he doesn't do too often, but was extremely effective for stress relief.

He gave some commands to my sub-conscious that I didn't understand but my whole body began to tremble. I felt ripples of energy moving up and down my body and then to my surprise I could actually feel the stress lifting off me. It felt as though it was sending my body into spasms as layer upon layer of stress and unhappiness was released. At certain points, I could feel the events that caused the pain. Some surprised me, others I fully expected.

As this process neared completion I began to feel an ominous sense of responsibility. It was as though I had just opened up a huge can of worms and I was now at the beginning of a very different way of being.

The fierce shaking subsided and my body came to a calmed rest.

"When I count to one, you will be totally awake and refreshed. Four, slowly waking up… three, your eyes are feeling lighter… two, open your eyes… one, you are now totally awake and refreshed, remembering everything that happened here. How do you feel?"

My mouth still didn't want to move and I felt as though I was floating a few feet off the bed. I was quite disorientated.

"Weird" was as much as I could muster.

I noticed how Christophe's voice had lost it's 'Godly' resonance. "I'm going to leave you for a few minutes to make a cup of tea and you'll need some time to recover ~ you've been through a lot so take it easy. Don't sit up until you're ready and don't even try to stand for at least ten minutes or you'll probably fall."

That crazy Sagittarian in me tried to get up after only a few minutes but I quickly discovered that just getting to a sitting position caused severe nausea.

I noticed the clock on the desk suggesting it had been an hour and a half from the time we began. I struggled to believe that as it felt like only 20 minutes or so had passed.

I felt strange, drugged almost. I decided not to attempt to stand so I sat wrapped up in the blanket, feeling very helpless.

The sweet fragrance of fruity herbal tea funnelled down the hallway, followed by the silhouette of Christophe who seemed to be much more animated.

Until this point he had been very 'business-like' and facial expressions had seemed awkward.

"Are you Ok?" he asked with sincerity.

"Yes" I said "Much better thanks – what a trip!"

He looked at me with an expression of understatement. "I don't come across many people who travel so far so quickly, you are extremely responsive" His whole face lit up and I sensed there was more to what he was saying, "If you're interested, I'd really like to do some exploring – it'll help both of us out. We'll go into as many past-lives as we can, look around, see what we can find."

I didn't see why not so we arranged to meet twice a week.

Christophe explained the reason for bringing me back when he did. "It concerned me that when I asked you to go to a happy time in your life, you kept going into the white light. For most people the happy place is an easy one to start off with and become familiar and relaxed with the process. Your response would suggest there are some very deep issues to deal with and the stress releasing process I did might help reach them." I didn't fully understand what he was saying, partly because I was still floating on my cloud but I knew it would all make sense later.

As an afterthought I asked "Were you pulling on my head and feet during that session?"

A smile snuck in as he explained, "No I wasn't but I'll tell you what it was. Your body became truly relaxed – probably for the first time in a very long time. When it does that, the whole spine straightens out on its own. I was watching for that as a sign to know when you were deep enough to begin. That's why we know that meditation is so good for the health – everything starts going back into its 'perfect place'".

I returned his smile then got up to leave. I still felt weak but fine enough to get home. I think I'll give work a miss today as well.

"Oh, and by the way…" he said as I stepped outside "No-one leaves this house without a hug." He stepped towards me and I quickly became lost amongst his massive body, now even more strong and supportive than ever.

"See you Wednesday, Thanks." I managed to say as I pulled from his embrace. A part of me didn't want to ever let go.

Being held by a man like that was not familiar to me so it was comforting, but awkward.

I drove the 30 minutes home in a daze and on pulling into my driveway I realised I couldn't remember any of the journey.

"Did I go through any red lights?" I wondered.

My mind flooded with thoughts and feelings, trying to get a grasp on the events of the last couple of days. Something had happened and I could feel it changing me, even as I sat in the car.

It seemed an eternity before I felt I wanted to even get out of the parked car. Logic prevailed and I made my way inside to make some lunch.

After some soup and a sandwich I felt much better, the food grounded me back into this world.

I decided to pop in to work, just to see how it was all going.

I felt amazingly refreshed on the drive to work. The sun was shining and I had a new sense of freedom about me. I felt strong and confident.

Things however were chaotic at work. I had a stack of messages from Board members wanting me to call them.

Here goes… "Hi Graeme, its Leigh. I just got your message to call."

There was a brief silence before he spoke "Yes. We were just wondering why you weren't at the club."

I could feel something stirring within me as I answered, "I had some things to take care of. Why, is there a problem?"

Again an awkward pause "Well it's just that you weren't there last night either."

This time something snapped inside me. I knew he had no clue of what had happened to me yesterday, and I knew he had no idea that I typically worked 18 hour days, seven days a week but I responded simply "Graeme, I would like you to take this as my verbal notice of resignation. Is one month enough time for you to find someone else?"

I couldn't believe what I had just done. It had almost happened
by itself. All my life I had been taught about financial stability and how important it was to maintain independence and security through a career so this was a huge shock, even to me.

"Umm, umm…" came down the phone.

"I can find someone to replace me if you'd like" I suggested.

He finally gathered himself together and I could feel he didn't want to take responsibility for this one. "One month is fine, but how about you meet with us next Monday at our Trust meeting and we can talk some more."

I could tell he really didn't know what to do or say so I humoured him "Sure." I knew without a doubt I was doing the right thing and nothing they said would change the way I was feeling.

I followed up a few other calls, arranged staff for the night then headed home. I was supposed to meet up with Mark tonight, although I wasn't in much of a clubbing mood but I had no way of letting him know. I couldn't call him at home because of his wife and he didn't want to risk the guys at his working knowing either.
I knew if I just didn't show up that he would call in to see me on his way home from the bar. I decided to see how I felt later.
It seemed as if the bar scene wouldn't pacify me any more.

I pulled into the driveway and noticed my Father's car. He was home early.

We had bought the house together about a year ago.

I had always adored my Father, which had caused major grief for my Mother. She was definitely the one who took hands-on care of my two brothers and myself as we grew up. She was left to administer punishment and I'm sure she was very hurt to see me adore my Father so much when in her mind all he contributed to our childhood was money.

She wanted him to have a more active roll in our upbringing. I still remember the arguments my parents would have before they finally split up.

I would see my Mother's desperation at trying to communicate with this person who had just shut off and wouldn't respond. I felt her pain in those moments and wondered why my Father just couldn't talk to her.

My Mother was now living in England with a wonderful man who did talk to her, and my Father was in and out of relationships.

I'm not sure if buying the house together was for his benefit or mine. His because he liked to be close to family, or mine as an attempt to put some stability or security in my life.

I had always been the 'black sheep' of the family. I didn't necessarily feel like I needed the stability of a home as for some reason I never felt as though I had had one or that I really belonged here, but it seemed like a good idea at the time.

"Hi Dad, you're home early" I said as I laid my keys on the dining room table.

He looked pale and tired. Seeing my father like that took me straight back to when I was 13.

My older brother Stuart would take me to school on his motorbike and we would come home some days for lunch. I think the real reason was more about being able to squeeze one more bike ride in to the day, because we could have taken our lunch to school or bought it there like most of the other kids.

Anyway on this particular day, we got home to find our

Father there. He was never normally home during the day because of such a long commute to work. We went about our business of getting lunch, noticing that he looked awful. He sat at the table writing what appeared to be a letter. His face was pasty white and it seemed to have broken out with a rash.
Stuart and I hurried back to school only to find when we returned home at the end of the day, the note our father had left. It let us know he was leaving. Leaving!
I remember that moment as it shocked me to the core.
I was overcome with a sensation of numbness that was like being in a bottle with all the air being sucked out quickly.
How could he leave us? I was devastated. We called our Mother at work who tried to sound shocked, but looking back now I realise she must have known.
She came straight home to talk to us. I remember bawling and telling her I wanted him to come home.
She piled us all in to the car and we drove around an area she thought he might be, determined to find him but with no luck.

Although we didn't find him that day, conversations with our Mother over the phone brought him back about a week later. One of the strangest feelings I have had was when he arrived home and knocked on the front door. It just didn't feel right. It was his house too.

Those memories seemed relevant somehow now as I looked at him standing in the kitchen, and I wondered what kind of stress he was under to have the effect it was on him.
"Yeah, decided to have an early day" was all he would give. I didn't push him. Although I would love to be able to help in any way I could, I would wait for him to open up to me.
"I'm quitting my job." I said.
"What?" He looked genuinely shocked and disappointed.
"I've been under too much stress, I have to stop"
Still not really believing it he asked, "What are you going to do - do you have another job lined up?"
"No" I replied slowly, knowing he would have a hard time understanding. "I'm not sure what I'm going to do yet, all I know is that I have to quit".

I could see thoughts of 'How is she going to pay the mortgage?' etc racing through his mind but I let it go. I knew he wouldn't push much further with it either.

I had begun to feel semi-normal by nine o'clock that night so I decided to meet up with Mark. He was waiting with a few of his buddies when I turned up at the bar. They had already had a few drinks so Mark was primed and ready to dance.

I decided to put the last couple of days behind me and let go. I drank up the kahlua Richard bought me and headed out to the floor to 'dance the night away'.

I needed five more kahluas before I totally relaxed and began enjoying myself. At only one point of the night did we have to separate, which was considered a good night.

Every once in a while someone Mark's wife knew would come in to the club. If one of Mark's buddies were close I would put my arms around him to look like we were a couple. They probably never questioned it anyway because they saw me there all the time with these guys.

Richard was desperately searching for that 'special one' but without much luck. He was one of those 'nice guys' that women just aren't immediately attracted to, or at least not in the shallow environment that we hung out in. He was Mark's best friend and quite often was the one to save the day.

One night recently Mark's wife Gloria came in. It totally shocked Mark as it was out of character for her. I was sitting between Mark and Richard and it seemed obvious I was with Mark but I grabbed Richard and begin kissing him passionately to make up for the compromising situation Gloria had caught us in. This drove Mark crazy. So much so that he had to walk out with Gloria.

A couple of days later as I was at the bar ordering a drink I was tapped on the shoulder. I spun around expecting Mark, but was instead surprised to see his ex-wife.

Tamsin was around six-foot tall, blonde, sophisticated and very beautiful. I had often wondered what had brought the two of them together as they seemed to come from different worlds. I was used to seeing her as she often came in to the club with her new husband but she had never spoken to me before.

"You know the reason our marriage didn't work was because of Mark's infidelity and if you think he'll be any different for you you're kidding yourself. He'll always do it. He's doing it with you, and if he's with you, there'll be someone else."

At least she was polite about it and in a way I respected her for telling me that.

All I could think of at the time was, "I know, it's convenient right now, that's all."

I'm sure she thought I was a 'home-wrecker' or something, but I hadn't gone into the relationship knowing he was married. He failed to tell me that for a long time, and by that point we had been seeing each other for a couple of years.

He told me that I was the one who had set him up with his wife, although I don't remember it at all as it was during a time I was drinking my way out of life and couldn't even remember Mark in my life at that time. So, I should have known he was married! That was his excuse anyway.

That alone had brought home to me how messed up my life was.

What makes people numb themselves to the world? I had had some abusive relationships, but I thought I had dealt with them. I had never had a strong, healthy relationship with my Mother, but that's not too unusual. I didn't know, but the more I began to question things, I realised I was finally ready to face whatever demon was haunting me.

"Are you ready?" Mark whispered in my ear as he nibbled on my neck.

I turned around in my chair to kiss him. "Very" We made our way back to my place.

It is a wonderful feeling to have totally 'unattached' sex.

I sometimes thought this is how most guys must feel when they pick up a girl for the night. No commitment to do it again, just pure fun. I knew I was using Mark and although by nature it made me feel a little guilty, I got over it quickly when he got up in the middle of the night to go home to his wife.

I never pried as to why he continued to do it, as that would be getting too personal and I didn't want to go there. It was perfect the way it was.

After Mark had snuck out into the crisp spring night I lay there thinking, "What is my life all about?" The effects of the alcohol had well worn off and I was left alone with myself again. I was too wired from the night so all I could do was think about me and who I really was. I felt different, although I had always felt different - why was that? The whole way through school I only ever really had one close friend. I knew everyone else saw me as different as well, but why? Why had I never fit in? Why did I feel a stranger at home even? Those years of demanding to know from my Mother who my real family was must have driven her crazy. I believed I must have been adopted into this family because it just didn't feel right. I knew they weren't my real family. Why did I look out of my bedroom window at the stars every night as a child, crying, asking 'them' - whoever 'they' were, to come and take me home? And who were those people in my bedroom at night, talking to me until I fell asleep?

The myriad of thoughts and questions I had tried for the last few years to block out were back, and it seemed with vengeance. My mind swirled with confusion and chaos until I slowly drifted into a deep sleep.

I heard a faint whisper "Leigh…" I wondered who would possibly be calling me. Perhaps Mark had come back. "Leigh…" This time was a little louder. My head then felt as though it was exploding as the voice rang through my body. Shaking every cell into life, "Leigh, it's time!" It commanded, almost shouting.

My eyes sprang open as I looked around in shock to see who was there. As my vision adjusted to the dark room I realised no one was there and that I had been sleeping.

It had been many years since I had had that same experience. When I was seven or eight years old I recall being woken many times by my name being called out. No one was ever there.

My body slowly recovered from the shock of being woken that way and I was able to drift into an uninterrupted sleep.

2 IT'S STARTING TO BRIGHTEN UP

The next day at work was uneventful. I focused on clearing up things to make life easier for someone new coming in to the job.

Like clockwork, the first patrons began to turn up at around five PM. Carol and Bob were the first to show as always. Not a day went by that I didn't see them there. I often wondered what else they did with their lives to drink like that every day of the week.

My day ended at 1am as usual and I was relieved not to have any plans to go out.
Once at home I quickly showered and went straight to bed. I wanted to experiment with self-hypnosis as Christophe had suggested.

I made myself comfortable, making sure I was warm enough, and then I began the same process Christophe had done the previous day. Right up through my body, from the tips of my little toes to the top of my head, meticulously I went through relaxing each muscle until I felt myself floating. What a wonderful feeling!

I allowed myself to feel this for a few minutes before I began to feel my body distort.

It took a lot of trust to allow this process, as it was such a strong and strange sensation.

I then began using commands I had heard Christophe use; telling myself to go deeper and deeper into the light.

I slowly began to ascend into a brilliant light, although it wasn't just a light, it was a feeling too. Total joy, love and bliss encompassed me.

Suddenly it all felt familiar to me. Somehow I knew this was where I belonged.

I continued going deeper and deeper into the light until I lost all sense of who I was.

After moving rapidly through corridors of golden light I became part of a 'brilliant light', at one with it. My mind raced to grasp some understanding of what I was experiencing. It was everything, yet nothing.

It didn't take too much to realise that what I was experiencing was well beyond anything that I could put into words. As I relaxed into this 'God Force' an amazing light appeared. It shimmered with every conceivable colour and as it moved closer to me it began to take the form of a golden 'glow'.

The most beautiful man I had ever seen then stood before me. He appeared old and yet young at the same time. Light danced from his eyes that transformed my heart to mush in an instant.

I felt so much Love from and for this man that I became aware of why I had felt so 'unloved' throughout my life. Nothing that I had experienced of 'Love' could come anywhere near this.

I felt my body then fall to my knees and I remembered something from the bible I had learnt at Sunday school as a child about kneeling before God.

Over the years as my attitudes changed I had thought it wasn't about bowing to God as we were all equal, and yet here I was on my knees. In that moment I realised what that scripture must have meant. It was that the presence of these incredible beings is so immense it forces you to your knees.

I looked upon this man before me with his perfect features and long flowing hair. I realised I knew him. He is my protector, my Father, my Lover, my Brother. This is Christ.

At my revelation he smiled and introduced himself to me as Sananda, and explained that he is the 'Christ Essence', one that all 'light'-beings and workers carry also. He told me that it is the same as what I carry within me. He explained that Jesus was the name he used while he was manifest on earth but in the form he is in now, he uses the name Sananda. He confirmed feelings I had of him being around me throughout my life.

In that moment I wondered if it was because of him and his perfection that had made me feel let down by most men.

Throughout my life I had felt as though 'Mr Right' or my 'Soul Mate' was not going to be with me this time and I knew and expected to be, or feel alone for most of my days.

"It's time for you to awaken." he said with words that danced upon the light.

The sensation that came with the words caused my entire being to tremble. It felt as though the words were coming from the very depth of my soul, making my Essence or Spirit jump to attention. I felt alive and invigorated.

"You have an important job to do" Again the words rang true to my Soul and I felt every cell in my body begin to tremble with delight. "You are going to experience an intense time of training whereby your vibration is going to be accelerated. The most important thing for you to do from now on is 'Trust'. You will be lead to do many different things in different ways that will be in preparation for your work to come. Your guidance will come through your intuition, so trust in yourself. Awareness's will be coming to you through insights and new concepts. These are not new to your 'True Self'; you have merely forgotten them in this incarnation. We, the Council of Light, will be assisting you in the removal of the 'veil', to lift you above the denseness of the third dimension. You are part of the 'Brotherhood of Light' and chose to come back to a human life to help the planet raise its consciousness. We are here for your guidance and support, so call upon us when you need to."

With that I felt an amazing embrace of light.

Gratitude, blessings and compassion flowed from his heart into mine. This was the family I had been missing. Finally all those questions that had plagued me for years began to be answered.

As his individual light began to meld back in to the 'whole', I reluctantly knew it was time to go back in to my body. I didn't want to go back, everything within me screamed out "No!" but I knew I had to. I had made a commitment.

I suddenly realised I had lost all sense of identity. I had no idea if I was male, female, my name or where I lived.

The confusion I felt in this moment was overwhelming and a sense of panic set in until gradually bits and pieces came back to me, and before I knew it I was back in my body, in my bed, female, Leigh, … Falling asleep.

It was a week later when I began putting the last of my belongings from the office into my car.

I had managed to advertise, interview and place a new manager within a week.

That was an interesting experience in itself. I found that most applicants were men and middle aged. There were a couple who were in their 50's who walked out on their interview when they saw me. They couldn't bring themselves to be interviewed by a young woman.

Brian had been the applicant the Trust Board had approved of after I narrowed it down to five possibilities. Although he would have been my last option, as I thought he was quite crass and unreliable to a certain degree, I was easily able to accept the decision and walk away with no regrets.

Brian came stumbling out of the building with my ergonomic chair "Are these things really any good?" he asked.

I smiled as I told him "They are if you have back problems" I reflected on how lucky I was to be standing.

I had done a lot of damage to my back as a child. I don't recall the exact situation but my Mother relayed it to me a couple of years ago. I had been swimming in a river and as the other kids were diving in I thought I'd have a go. Apparently my efforts resulted in my head connecting with a rock. There was no obvious damage right away but I gradually began losing my vision.

I remember the doctor saying months later, "There's nothing much we can do other than to provide glasses for a while and I'll refer you to a school to learn Braille."

The extent of what that meant never truly sank in as a child.

About a year later as my Mother became more involved with alternative medicines and spirituality, she took me to a chiropractor where I went through a series of adjustments and gradually got my vision back. A dull throbbing back and neck ache however did remain.

As my Mother also suffered with back pain, my claims of discomfort where often overlooked as 'just copying' her, and not believed so I spent a lot of time in constant pain.

There were many times during school that my headaches were so severe that visiting the chiropractor a couple of times a day was not uncommon.

Anyway, this first accident was followed by numerous falls from horses, physical abuse and a motorcycle accident that should have taken my life without a second thought.

I was in my 'self-destruct' days ~ well, more than normal actually. I really didn't like myself or anyone else very much. I had become involved with the Hell's Angels, or rather they had latched on to me. At the time it was exciting to be racing around the country on Harley Davidsons with a group of people who seemed to be respected everywhere they went, something I felt was lacking in my life. It was the perfect way for me to punish and hurt myself, but for what I didn't know.

I began going out with Richard who was very soft and caring compared to most of them. Mostly we would meet at the headquarters for nightly parties.

I gained an enemy quickly after beating him at a game of pool.

I hadn't seen this guy around much and had no idea how bad his temper was but as soon as I sunk the black ball he raced over to me, put his hand around my throat, picked me up off the floor and pushed me against the wall.

"Don't ever do that again," he said.

He demanded we play another game, which I tried to lose, but it seemed the more I tried to play badly, the easier the balls went in. This time as I sunk the black I quickly made my way into the other room to the protective arms of Richard vowing never to play another game of pool there.

A couple of weeks after splitting up with Richard I bumped into some of the club members at their regular weekend pub.

John, who had always been nice, asked if he could talk to me.

He led me to a room in the house next door and once the door was shut he pushed me to the bed and held a knife to my throat. I was told not to make a sound as he raped me. It was surreal and I didn't really believe he was doing this to me. I struggled as much as I could and told him not to be such a jerk. I told him that I thought he was a nice guy and if sex was what he wanted, he could've tried another way.

I felt the knife slice into my neck and a trickle of warm blood finding its way to settle in the hollow above my collarbone.

"Shut up!" he growled.

Unable to find a safe way out of the situation, I took myself into the familiar inner worlds I often used as an escape.

I decided to move to the south island for six months to get away from everything.

I had met a lot of people from all over the country through the bike club and contacted some of them when I arrived in Christchurch.

Peter's long brown hair and facial features reminded me of something familiar, and I realised he looked a lot like Sananda; which would explain the strong attraction to him.

We hit it off quickly, and despite my cautiousness of bikers, I trusted him. Our relationship was going strong after six months.

After a private party at a bar, I got on Peter's motorcycle despite not having a spare helmet. He hadn't expected me to show up as I didn't think I was going to get out of work in time. I insisted he wear his helmet and agreed it would be a safe enough ride, so we left.

The rain was pelting down and I had to snuggle as close as I could to Peter with my head buried in his back to avoid the raindrops that felt like rocks with embedded razor blades on my face at 80kph.

Halfway home as we went through a major tunnel connecting Lyttleton to Christchurch, we came upon a police roadblock. I have no idea what made Peter panic but we sped right through the block with all other 50 bikes right behind us.

The traffic officers quickly pursued.

It all happened so quickly and yet I viewed it in slow motion. An incredible gut-wrenching sick feeling overwhelmed me as I was thrown over both the handlebars and Peter. A blur of lights, then darkness enveloped me as I was spun like a rag doll from the hands of a bad tempered child.

I landed on the motorway with my wrists instinctively trying to protect my head from the inevitable crash and roll.

Several more rolls and a hundred-metre slide along the slick surface left me sitting on the edge of the road. The slippery roads were my saving grace that kept me from horrendous physical damage.

Dazed and winded I became aware of settling in to a sitting position on the curb, unable to move or breathe. It seemed humorous to me in that moment that the position I was now in was the same as when I was on the bike.

I was just beginning to piece the events of the previous few minutes together when a police car flew past me, shaking my body helplessly in its wake. I was unable to move, still winded and in shock.

An eternity seemed to pass before a group of girls I had met at the party stopped. They picked me up and managed to manoeuvre me into their car. We wound up at the bike club headquarters where many members were talking excitedly about the chase and boasting how no one had been caught.

Meanwhile Peter's body was being removed from the tangled mess that had been created from the impact. The girls related as much as they could about what they had seen at the crash site.

Over the next few hours I found out we had hit a parked car on the motorway travelling at over 100kph. It was like a 'head-on'.

The car we hit had broken down, but the owners had left it sitting in the fast lane with no lights on.

Instead of the common action of the rider being thrown over the bike, the handlebars had caught Peter and he was pinned between the car and what was left of his bike. He didn't have a chance.

"Is that why you use it?" I heard, which jolted me back to the inquisitive face of Brian who was now next to me trying to squeeze the chair into my car trunk.

He was not an attractive man, physically or mentally. He came across immediately with an exuding arrogance that could only bring compassion from me as I wondered what battles he was fighting in his life to cause him to put on that type of front.

"Yes" I replied after a moment. I had become so immersed in the memories I had almost forgotten what we were talking about.

"I had a few accidents and my spine's been a little knocked around. The chair really helps though."

"Will it ever get better?" he asked with genuine interest.

"Well after my last accident it's actually bent and twisted in all the wrong ways, some pieces of bone have been chipped off and I'm told it is riddled with scoliosis. One specialist wanted me to have the 'fusion' operation where they would take some bone from my thigh and fuse it onto my spine, but it's not really recommended at my age so I gave it a miss. I'm still standing though, despite being told I'll have to spend my life in a wheelchair."

He looked surprised, "Really?"

I continued by telling him how I had lost my faith in doctors.

"I know what you mean," he replied, "You certainly hear of some horror stories out there."

I was drawn back into the memory of the accident, back to the biker's headquarters I was taken to after the accident. Unable to walk, the girls took me into a room and placed me in a bed to rest for the night.

My mind was still not clear although I felt I should have been going to the hospital instead of this place. My right hip was in a lot of pain and this was aggravated as the girls changed my clothes. I noticed my jeans were in shreds as they peeled them off me.

I wasn't able to sleep with the pain I was feeling and I was becoming quite concerned about Peter when a tall figure came into the room.

It was dark but I knew it was a biker, as I could smell his 'leathers'. I thought he was coming in to check on me but he proceeded to undress and tell me he was going to 'take care of me'.

I told him he was crazy and tried to scream but he placed his huge, powerful hand over my mouth.

The pain in my hip now seemed to be a distant memory as I took myself into another place. I surrendered; helpless again. This man was big and strong with obviously no conscience. Any resistance from me was useless.

The memories of that experience became too painful to deal with so I shut them down and headed back inside the club with Brian to do one last check around for anything I might have missed. I didn't want to come back unless I absolutely had to.

I wrote my phone number on a piece of paper for him, telling him that if there was anything urgent he could give me a call and I'd try to help.

The last week and a half had gone by very quickly. Uneventful for the most part with the odd, very scary moment as the fear and uncertainty monsters reared their heads. I still had no idea what I was going to do or how I would pay next month's mortgage.

3 THE TRANSITION

My time off work was well needed and my visits to Christophe had opened up understandings of many issues in my life. I began to understand my connections with family through past lives and the whole role karma plays into it. I finally read a couple of books I had previously tried to read for years but never really had the time.

I also discovered a wonderful little shop called 'Rainbow Network'. It was a metaphysical shop that along with the usual crystals, incense, etc, had an amazing library.

I ploughed through as many of those books as I could, sometimes one a day. I was thirsty for a connection to something and this newly evolving spiritual path seemed to be it. I felt comfortable with it.

The information I was reading wasn't new to me. It was as if reading the words was merely reminding me of what I already knew. I found I could discern easily what I felt was and wasn't true to me. I took it all for what it was.

By the fifth week I had exhausted the book supply. I had grown tired of the whole bar scene and of Mark too. He had noticed this change in me as well and wasn't too surprised when I told him I needed to end our affair.

It was an easy parting from what was the 'easiest' relationship yet.

I progressively began to feel stagnant. I had a lot of pressure on me from my father about my future. He normally understood my different and totally unconventional ways and over the years had developed an interest in spiritual things as well. We often talked about what I was going through and I tried to describe the visions I was having as a result of all the meditation I had been doing. He encouraged me on all these things, but money was a whole different ball game.

I succumbed to the fear and scoured the papers for a job.

I didn't really want to go back into the bar scene but one particular job wouldn't go away. I went for the interview just because I knew I was qualified and it would boost my ego a bit to turn it down.

Once there however, I felt different and a strong feeling within encouraged me to take the job.

It was a meaningless Bar Manager job that in all honesty, they really didn't need, but I worked on making some minor improvements and passed my time away while questioning the whole purpose of it.

One of the casual bartenders caught my attention. I felt as though I recognised her in some way.

Jenny seemed to light up as she talked to me and we became good friends. We talked about our spiritual beliefs and she told me that when the company had put my photo up on the board, she had immediately recognised me as someone she had known in a past life or something.

I went to her house and met with her husband and two children. Roy, her husband, was curious about our beliefs and claims but was happy when he could challenge and question us. He would separate us and would have us come in to the room one by one when he would ask, "What colour is my aura?" I would respond that it was yellow. Jenny would come in next and she would see the same colour as me every time. Roy would look at us claiming we had used signals to let each other know what we were going to say.

No matter what we did or said, he was able to find fault. We didn't mind though as we weren't trying to prove anything to him. We were really excited that we had found someone we could relate to on this spiritual level.

We decided to meet regularly and practice techniques such as clairvoyance, e.s.p. and anything else that might interest us. In the meantime the company we worked for was having some major financial problems, and being one of the last employed, I was one of the first to be laid-off. I couldn't believe it.

At such short notice I wasn't able to put any savings away to help out for a while.

Things were not going so well at home. My younger brother had moved in without my knowledge. My father had decided that he could help out with the rent. I was really angry with him for not communicating to me about it but it was clear that he was there to stay.

I filled Dad in with what had transpired at work, which didn't go down very well. I tried again to talk about my feelings but he shut down immediately so I told him I wanted out. I felt as though he had totally disrespected me and placed no value on my partnership or role in the property. I went to bed feeling depressed.

The following morning I made a trip to the store to get the paper. Now I needed a house and a job, things were not looking good. I picked up a lotto ticket as well.

The paper revealed a small 2brm cottage for rent that was available the following week. I had no deposit money but decided I would take it.

It was old and not in very good shape but was secluded amongst some beautiful trees and had a small creek running through the bottom of the property.

I filled in all the forms and promised I'd be back on Monday with the deposit. Now I just had to work out where that would come from. My father was an unlikely person to help out as he was barely talking to me.

That night I decided to go along to a meditation evening I had heard about. I had no idea what to expect but things could only get better at this point.

I arrived ten minutes early and met Lisa who would be running the evening. Her voice was soft and soothing as she introduced herself to me, and her house was warm and inviting.

A group of about fifteen others were already seated and were busy chatting away to each other. We all exchanged greetings and I took my place in the closest chair.

I sat quietly listening to conversations about Ramtha, astrology, earth changes and certain family members causing all sorts of upheavals, while Lisa moved around quietly shutting off lights and unplugging the phone.

A tape recorder was turned on and tested before Lisa noticed my obvious unease,

"What I normally do is when I feel ready to start, we all just close our eyes, go into a meditation and then I'll bring through the words from the light-beings with us."

"Ok" I said with a reassuring smile although still not really knowing what to expect.

Soon the room came to a still hush as each person observed Lisa's readiness. They all made themselves comfortable; some removing sweaters, some putting them on along with socks.

I closed my eyes and began my process for relaxation although after only a minute I noticed I felt far more relaxed than any previous meditation.

"Greetings" rang the first words, "Ashtar with you"

I was amazed with the clarity that I saw visions of beautiful beings of white light before me. I felt myself being lifted up beyond my body, beyond the planet, to a chamber. Surrounded by a pearly white light, I was totally unaware of Lisa's voice.

I was now on my own journey.

The beings introduced themselves as being of the 'Council of Light' and referred to me a number of times as a 'light-worker'. They told me of this great 'Council' that is looking over the planet, assisting in its transformation. They explained that a part of the 'Light worker's' responsibility was to anchor the higher light vibrations to Earth. This was done through the process of being worked-on individually to remove old ways, conditionings, habits etc and making room within the form or body to store this higher, pure energy or vibration.

This energy was then transferred to the earth through being present and part of this ongoing process. It was now time that I began to prepare for my work ahead.

I was excited. I had felt so much anticipation of purpose throughout my life. At seven or eight years old I was often frustrated at the fact I had to wait to grow up. I felt there was something important I needed to do and couldn't comprehend why I had to wait. There were occasions when I set out to do just that, but to my disappointment and total confusion, I was brought back and told never to 'run away' again.

These beings were familiar to me and I began to regard them as family. They asked me if I'd like them to show me around their 'vessel'.

The 'vessel' was huge. It had glowing soft walls and corridors that were alive as we moved through them effortlessly, gliding or floating. The first room we came to was large and not unlike a lecture room. It was filled with both children and adults, learning.

"These people come during their sleep states where they are refreshed and reconnected with their 'true selves' and purpose." One told me.

I realised that the communication going on was telepathic and the more I accepted everything going on, the more I knew.

I could feel that there were many more rooms just like the one we were standing in.

Next we stopped at what looked like the 'control room'. It was busy with beings moving around. A huge screen was in the centre of the room and one of the beings standing next to it approached me. Although they appeared androgynous I felt I needed to refer to him as a 'him'. He greeted me as 'Commander' and asked if I'd like to see the engine room.

"I'd love to" I said, feeling comfortable with the telepathic communication.

We moved down through a series of corridors and stairs to a room full of equipment that reminded me of a ship's engine room. I was aware of a huge sense of pride coming from this being. He was responsible for its functions; some of which brushed my awareness but held such intricacies I was unable to grasp consciously. I was shown with great excitement and passion some of the outstanding features that had been his creation.

When he finished showing me his work I thanked him for sharing and expressed my pride in his work.

Back up on the top levels, we passed by many more rooms with a variety of different functions. I noticed a healing room ahead and observed many people drifting in and out. It was such a serene place I thought I'd like to spend more time there.

Instantaneously my thought was acknowledged and I was told, "Now that you've been here you can return whenever you like." I thanked them for showing me around and I was informed the Council was waiting for me.

I was transported to the door of a large round room where eleven beings were seated around a large circular table, waiting.

They welcomed me as if they'd known me for a very long time.

"We are the 'Brotherhood,'" the one closest to me said.

He was very tall, robed in a plain gown that was luminescent with an amazing sash of light over his shoulder. I sensed an incredible amount of beauty, wisdom and power in the room. They were all similarly dressed although I couldn't make out features. They appeared to be fluid light, in form. I never got a strong sense of whether they were male or female either but I was overwhelmed with a sense of belonging.

They asked me to take my seat as one of the twelve and we would begin.

Discussions began about Earth. Plans were made for certain events and things to be done. There was talk of other places as well, outside earth and it's galaxy as well as my role in all of it. At that point I began to loose my focus. Things began to get hazy and I was aware of being pulled down.

I realised I was moving back in to my body when I heard Lisa's voice telling us to be totally present within the body. I took my time coming out of the meditation, as I didn't want the sensation to end.

I felt an aliveness I had never felt before, or in this life at least. I wriggled my fingers and toes to really ground my energy back in to the body and gradually opened my eyes.

Most of the others had returned and were sitting patiently for us stragglers before discussing their experiences.

I sat in a state of pure bliss and joy while my consciousness tried to grasp what had happened and piece it all together. Once everyone was back and had opened their eyes, Lisa got up to prepare a cup of tea.

"That was really wonderful," I told her as I helped set out the teacups.

"Oh, great" she said with a huge smile.

"I can't remember any of what was said though"

Lisa laughed when I told her this and she explained that it was quite common, which is one of the reasons she tapes the sessions; "so we can listen to or read it later". She offered to send me a copy of it. I jumped at the opportunity,

"That would be wonderful"

I described as best as I could what I had experienced and Lisa was excited for me. I decided I would continue coming to these meetings every two weeks from now on.

I was on a high during the drive home with energy buzzing around my head and the presence of the light beings still strongly around me.

The following Sunday I routinely checked my lotto ticket to find I had won $500; the exact amount I needed as a deposit for the house. I felt utterly blessed and protected.

I proudly handed it over on Monday to the real estate agent and began moving in to my new place.

Life had become fascinating, with major changes going on. I had made a commitment to my spiritual pathway and things began revealing themselves to me.

I had to stop the hypnosis sessions because I no longer had an income and I was gaining such insight through self-hypnosis and meditation, I felt I no longer needed it.

I was such a great subject for Christophe that during one session, he made the suggestion for me to go into the future. I felt myself moving forward but my mind kicked in and questioned whether I really wanted to go there yet. It just didn't feel right. I felt as though I was treading on sacred ground and perhaps I shouldn't, so I brought myself out of the 'trance'.

I understood that he was probably just excited about the discoveries he was making through our process together and wanted to take it to another level, but I felt he should have discussed it with me first.

I had achieved so much from the regression work.

The first time Christophe told me to go to a situation with my mother, I just cried. Every time I was taken to issues surrounding my mother I would cry and felt such emotional pain I would have to be brought out of the session. Through these experiences however, I realised how much I had wanted to be close to my mother growing up, but it never happened.

During one of the sessions I felt myself in my mother's womb. She was about seven months pregnant with me and I felt an overwhelming sadness. I felt unwanted and abandoned. When Christophe prompted me to find out more I discovered that my parents had had an argument and my mother felt a sense of hopelessness at that point and had considered taking her life.

At the moment of my birth I remember feeling a wave of dread ripple right through my being. I sensed a 'love-less' life.

My mother strengthened these feelings of being unwanted by her absentness. Quite often she would be in another head place.

I don't think she really wanted to be here and was dealing with her own emotional pain at the time, but as a child I didn't understand that. I just wanted her to love me but I never felt as if she really did.

On top of all this spiritual work I was doing I had to deal with chronic financial problems. I was unable to find a job, not through lack of trying but more due to Divine intervention.

I decided to begin a spiritual development group, not only for my own benefit, but now that I had a basic understanding of how it worked I wanted to share it with as many people as possible.

I placed small free ad in the paper and drew up some signs that I placed on notice boards around the area.

A consistent group of people came to my house every week and we did basic psychometry and clairvoyant exercises as well as a meditation. I felt inspired as more and more in the group began to trust in their intuition and became equally excited.

One evening just as the weekly group had wound up I received a phone call from Christine who was a friend I had worked with at the Hotel.

"Peter's dead" she said. "He committed suicide"

Peter was one of the patrons we had become close to. At first I thought she was joking as he was the last person on earth I would think would do something like that. He was very handsome, funny, had a great job, plenty of friends, and it seemed not a care in the world.

Once it set in I was devastated. We had had a close relationship for about six months a couple of year's prior, and the whole situation now seemed surreal.

I went to the funeral a couple of days later, meeting up with some familiar faces.

I got the chance to talk with Christine and Sarah about what I was doing with my life now. Sarah took an interest in the spirituality and was keen to come to some of my groups.

Eventually we learned of the trauma in our mutual friend's life that had driven him to such drastic measures, and it made all of us review the many issues in our own lives.

This was the first person I knew who had taken their life, but in a weird way I understood why. I had considered it many times myself.

There were points in my life that I felt so alone and helpless to change anything, I couldn't see any purpose in being alive and I was sure no one would miss me.

Luckily on one occasion when I took the thoughts a bit further, my method failed and I wound up with a bad headache and nausea after a handful of pills let me down.

Sarah and I formed a close relationship over the following weeks. She would arrive early for the group each week, which enabled us an opportunity to catch up on our individual spiritual experiences throughout the week and generally share what we were feeling.

Jenny lived quite a distance away so never made it, although I still visited her regularly and we continued to be led by our guides and helpers through many discoveries of the Self and the Universe. We experimented with taking photos of the energies in the room with us.

One evening after our meditation we were discussing what we had each experienced and I was sitting on the table facing the hallway while Jenny was on the other side of the table facing me. I began to see something in the hallway behind Jenny but didn't say anything as I thought I was just seeing spirit, which wasn't uncommon. Gradually however, this 'entity' began to manifest.

It was the first time I had seen anything like it. It wasn't necessarily human. I wasn't really sure what it was.

I wasn't scared or concerned at all, more curious. I waited until it had almost fully manifested there in the hallway before motioning Jenny to turn around. She turned and screamed at the sight of the 'entity' standing there.

It vanished pretty quickly but at least she had seen it as well. It probably wasn't the best way to make her aware of it but I didn't seem to have much control over the process. I knew that seeing this entity that way was part of my consciousness expansion.

Through transfiguration we were taken into other times and space.

During one particular evening we sat focusing on each other. Our faces began to transform and the energy in the room began to shift until no longer was it just our faces changing. It was now the whole room transforming, as if we had been transported to another world.

I felt as though I was seeing in to one of Jenny's past lives.

It looked like I was in a tent not unlike what you would see in an Arabian movie. The colours were vibrant to the point of being fluorescent. The surroundings seemed to be two-dimensional almost like a cartoon, yet the image of Jenny; who had transformed into a warrior, remained three-dimensional.

I could sense the texture of the textile rugs and animal skins which contrasted with the fine silk draping around the walls.

Weapons hung from the supporting beams within this elaborate desert tent. I was aware of everything surrounding her life at this time, including her title, mission, etc.

My senses felt as thought they were on overload. I could smell not only the environment I was in, but also something else. Something I couldn't grasp. It wasn't just a smell, in the sense that I could taste and feel it as well.

My mind was working overtime to grasp the reality of it all when I began to see Jenny's warrior head start disappearing into a brilliant ball of light. I felt as though we were being taken into yet another space or dimension. It was frightening on one level because at a certain point we realised there was the possibility we might not come back.

I had no problem with this possibility as I had nothing to lose, but Jenny had children so she pulled out. At that moment I felt us both being drawn back with the Arabian vision fading back into the couch and plainly wallpapered room.

It was an absolutely incredible experience and as we sat there in a state of shock at what had just transpired, we noticed the clock. It had been four hours since we sat down to begin the transfiguration. Four hours that felt like 30 minutes. Laughter then overcame us until we felt grounded again.

We became aware that the laughter was a huge and necessary release of the energy we had taken on or absorbed to be able to experience what we did.

My sleep that night was out-of-body and I woke up feeling hung over. I was beginning to learn about the physical effects of all this learning and exploring, and the necessity to drink plenty of water.

My spiritual group continued to thrive. I learnt so much during these evenings. We mostly did clairvoyant exercises whereby we 'tuned-in' to the spirit world, but everyone gained a real trust for their own intuition and guidance, which for me was what it was all about. I found I knew things instinctively. I knew about the importance of using light to protect myself before doing anything on the spiritual level, and I guided troubled entities back into the light without any of the typical fear surrounding these particular spirits.

My spiritual vision became stronger and clearer and I now frequently saw energies around me, both of 'spirit' and 'light-beings'. These light-beings were also present every time Jenny and I got together. They would often appear in the room, towering up to the ceiling with a vibrant bluish hue. They would stand with arms spread in a protective shield around us. Most of the time there were up to three of them. It seemed that they would 'open' up a space for our experience. We felt incredibly safe around them and trusted whole-heartedly their guidance.

Working with this by accepting and asking, tended to open up new awareness's and a much stronger knowing and trust within.

My financial situation was however a whole different story. With no financial support and the inability to get a job, I was struggling. It was emotionally tough because of my conditioning to be independent and being taught that your finances are the gauge of your success.

I received a small amount in the way of donations from the weekly group but not enough to survive. I was driven to beg for cigarettes as they were still a crutch and helped me deal with the stress. I felt trapped, alone, scared and helpless. My world was crashing in on me and I couldn't see a way out.

Over the next couple of months I went through what I perceived as Hell. I couldn't afford food for myself let alone my animals.

An Aunt dropped off a couple of bags of groceries to help out but I continued in this world of self-torture until I felt I couldn't go on any more.

I needed to get rid of possessions, they were weighing me down. I went through boxes of old photos and school certificates wondering what they all meant. I placed them, impartially in the fireplace and put a match to them.

Watching those memories twist and contort with the heat of the flame emphasised that there had to more to it all than these snap-shots of certain events that happened. Those memories remained, even without the piece of paper. My life had to be about an understanding or knowing. There was something much more valuable than those photos that I was missing and needed to feel. They were holding me back. Those memories were holding me in the past, which was a place of pain and confusion.

I began un-cluttering my house of everything unnecessary until there was nothing left but me. What a wake-up call! I wasn't even really sure who 'me' was.

My mind struggled to retain its identity based on my conditioning of what and who I thought I should be, but it caused me more pain with the memories it induced.

After a couple of days crying and feeling sorry for myself I was able to get to a point when the pain subsided. A stillness and peace came over me. There was no more of 'me' that I could lose. I had lost everything. So I surrendered completely.

Not knowing what or whom I was surrendering to, I placed my life in the hands of fate, declaring that if I should lose my life through starvation or a broken heart, it probably wouldn't be too bad after what I'd been through already and where I was now.

4 THE FIRST STEP OF A NEW LIFE

The ad read: 'Person needed to help out with two children. Housework, etc. Live-in Leigh. Call Mary.'

Something stood out about this ad. Maybe it was that it had my name on it, so I quickly called it.

"If you'd like, come up tomorrow so you can meet us and decide if it will work for you." Mary sounded excited. She hadn't received any calls up to this point and was starting to think no one would. I responded,

"That sounds great, I'll see you tomorrow around one o'clock." Hoping she wouldn't pick up on my over-eagerness.

Mary explained that she was three months pregnant with her fourth child and was not in good health. The doctors had ordered her to stay in bed until the birth. Her husband Barry, spent all day out working and any leisure time was spent fishing, so they desperately needed help with the other two children.

"The government will give us a wage for someone to help out. It won't be much but most of your expenses will be taken care of by us" Mary explained.

She sounded nice enough. It wasn't the type of situation I thought I would ever be in. I didn't consider myself to be good around kids, and living in a house full of strangers wasn't terribly inviting either. I was a loner and loved my privacy. But something had compelled me to call. It felt right.

The drive to Leigh took about an hour. It was a beautiful sunny day and the long winding road up the coast was peaceful and refreshing. I had been trapped in the city for so long, barely looking up long enough to see the ocean that had been only a mile from my home.

As I got closer to the small township of Leigh, I felt as if I was coming home. It felt very familiar to me.

A young boy of about five greeted me at the door.

"Hi. What's your name?" I asked the inquisitive face peering at me through the small crack in the door.

"Paul" he replied before turning and running, calling for his mother.

"Sorry about that, I was just having a rest. "Come in."

Mary's long red hair hung over her frail body that seemed to be in no shape at all to carry a baby. She reminded me of an anorexic, who's gaunt and skeletal body reeked of self-punishment and denial.

She led me in to the main living area of what appeared to be a large house. Huge windows looked out onto the harbour, giving a vast view of any marine activity.

The décor was simple. No fancy decoration, it was very typical of the 80's. A huge cactus consumed the western corner of the room where it was about to reach the nicotine-coated ceiling.

Paul was playing with some small toy cars with his younger brother who appeared to be around two years old.

"This is Tom" Mary proudly announced as she reached down to pick him up. "He's eighteen months old next month." "Would you like a cup of tea?" Mary asked, placing Tom back down next to a pile of toys. Tom however turned and made his way straight back to Paul and the exciting game of seeing how far the car would fly off a cardboard ramp.

"I'd love one." I replied as I got up to help prepare it.

A kitchen bar separated the living area and kitchen, which made the room feel very spacious while allowing you to keep an eye on the children or guests while cooking. Mary mentioned that she had asked Barry to stop in if he got a chance between jobs to meet me.

"He is an electrician, one of the few good ones in the area so he stays pretty busy."

We sat on the couch to carry on our conversation.

I filled her in on my past, not really knowing how to explain what I had been through during the past few months and luckily she didn't go there. I mentioned my spiritual beliefs and I was pleasantly surprised when she expressed an interest.

Mary then explained her situation and that she suffered from a liver and kidney disease. She had never carried a child to full-term but this pregnancy was by far the most dangerous. She also shared that her first child had died, considered to be cot death. It was such a common diagnosis at that time that it was almost accepted as natural.

We were getting along wonderfully.

At that moment I decided I would do it. I would move away from everything familiar to me, to a new town, new job, and new people, to a whole new life.

Suddenly Paul stopped what he was doing and looked up. His face lit up as he ran towards the kitchen.

"Dad's home!" he cried.

Minutes later a tall, dark-haired man entered the room and Mary introduced him to me.

"Hi. How are you? Sorry I only have a couple of minutes before I have to be at Mrs. Connolly's but I thought a couple of minutes was better than none." Barry quickly disappeared into the refrigerator to organise some lunch. He seemed nice enough as well. It looked like my luck was turning around.

I drove away from Leigh feeling liberated and excited as I scanned the new scenery that would become my new 'back-yard'.

Things had gone smoothly. Mary and I connected easily and the children didn't object to me in any way, in fact after an initial 'shy' period they wouldn't leave my side which not only surprised Mary but definitely me as well.

The only contact I had really had with children was with my younger cousins. I would baby-sit for them sometimes, but definitely not enough to feel comfortable.

I wondered how it would work being so far away from the city. I really wanted to continue with the meditations at Lissa's and it felt as if Jenny and I were just getting started with the learning we were doing together. Despite my questioning, I knew without a doubt it was what I had to do.

As soon as I walked in the door to my little house I picked up the phone and called Mary. I checked to make sure I could bring Jabez, Cling-on and Annie with me.

When she responded that it would be lovely to have some animals around I told her, "If you are interested in having me, I would love to move in and help you."

"Oh, wonderful" she replied. "When can you move up here?"

I hadn't considered this far ahead so I told her I'd have to see how much notice the real estate company would need on the house. "… but possibly a week or two at the most. Would that work for you?"

She assured me that would be fine and offered her husband to help me move anything, although the room was fully furnished so I wouldn't need to bring anything but myself and some clothes.

The real estate company informed me that one-week would be enough notice so I prepared to move. By this time I had begun some minor communications with my Father so I filled him in on my plans.

The next week was reasonably good. The security of this job allowed me to relax and spend some time just being. I spent many hours in meditation; something I hadn't been able to do a lot of while caught up in all the stress of my previous situation.

Clarity filled me and a new sense of direction flooded my being.

I let my friends know what I was up to and contacted everyone from the spiritual development group; informing them that the next meeting would be the last. I was a little sad to end such a wonderful thing. I had formed some wonderful friendships and gained amazing insights into the spiritual world in a very short amount of time.

I settled into my new environment easily. Everyone was easy to get along with, despite the children being way too hyperactive, a result of too much junk food. Mary and I spent many hours sitting around talking, drinking coffee and smoking cigarettes. Both she and Barry were chain smokers as well as their good friend Ralph who would drop in for five or six hours on a daily basis.

I managed to continue with Lisa's group and had been invited to attend her other one, which was a much smaller group where information was channelled. The purpose of it was to activate the 'light-worker' aspect within. I was of course honoured to be a part of it. I spent a lot of time in meditation and saying affirmations to encourage the 'wake-up' process. So now I was driving into the city every week.

I didn't see Jenny as much but we decided there was no reason we couldn't continue to work together, but apart.

To test our theory, we arranged to send a message to her husband Roy at a given time on a particular night. This message would be for him to have a piece his favourite candy that he always kept in the pantry.

This exercise would serve two purposes. Firstly it would allow us to see the connection we had and secondly it might give Roy that extra bit of proof he claimed he needed.

At ten o'clock on this pre-determined night I sat down and visualised a craving for the candy. I then sent it to Roy and visualised him going to the pantry for it. I spent about half an hour with this focus before going to sleep.

The following day I called Jenny and find out that Roy had indeed gone to the pantry but had run out of his favourite candy. He then got in the car and drove to the store to buy a new packet. We were amazed at how it had worked. Of course Roy didn't believe us. He claimed he was going to get some then anyway, but highly unlikely at that hour of the night. From then on Jenny and I began a series of long-distance telepathy exercises.

I started to see a lot more lights, shapes and images appearing. This light would often appear in a room while I was sitting quietly and would transform into shapes and objects. I felt the energy around me with more clarity. I began to sense things before they happened or sometimes I would be given insight as to why certain things happened.

My spiritual work and path had now definitely begun and I felt huge changes going on within myself. I knew that in order for me to become a pure, spiritual being, I would have a lot of work to do on myself. All of my conditioning, fears, etc. would have to be released, not to mention any past-life residue I may have brought with me. I was however, up for the challenge and feeling stronger each and every day as new awareness's and understandings came to light.

Things had been going smoothly for several months. I had given up smoking. In a chain-smoker's house none-the-less, and I was beginning to feel clarity like I had never felt before.

On my way to collect cigarettes from the store for Barry, I saw a very expensive car parked outside, which was uncommon for this area as most people had farm vehicles or old sedans. It wasn't a wealthy area by any means.

As I neared the doorway a tall older gentleman walked out, nearly bumping into me. Our eyes locked briefly in a state of recognition. The following seconds felt like hours as we watched each other continue on our paths.

For several days after I wondered what it had all been about.

A couple of days later during dinner, Barry got a call from someone wanting electrical work done. It was nothing too unusual except that I heard my name being mentioned. I sat in eager anticipation at what could have been said; having a gut feeling it was the mysterious man on the other end of the line. Chills ran through me as my 'Being' seemed delighted in what was unfolding.

"Well that was Michael. He needs some wiring done and has some plans he wants me to look over first."

As he was going to be working out of town tomorrow, Barry suggested that I drive up to collect them for him. My heart began pounding with excitement, or fear; I couldn't tell anymore.

I didn't sleep well at all that night but the following morning after walking Paul to school and sending Mary back to bed; which had become more difficult than looking after the children at times, I packed Tom and some lunch into the car and headed up the mountain to Michael's.

"If I followed the instructions properly, this should be it" I said to a totally uninterested Tom.

Pulling into the driveway revealed a picture-perfect house, white picket fence and all. It was a large white homestead-looking place, set amongst lush green farmland and grazed by small white goats. To the northeast was the most magnificent view I think I had ever seen. Rolling hills, ocean and a coastline that wouldn't quit. It reminded me of something out of a fantasy novel. I fell in love with the place instantly.

Michael came out to greet us along with his huge white, and very round Chow dog. Dressed comfortably in jeans and a cotton shirt, Michael reeked of class and sophistication.

Although we felt uncomfortable initially because of the obvious attraction, we had a wonderful afternoon, talking and drinking peppermint tea.

Michael was a photographer by trade. Being a very good photographer, he travelled back-and-forth to America where he had been living for six months of the year. He would do some location shoots for high-class automotive companies, then come back to run his goat farm.

He considered himself to be spiritual and was involved in a men's group in the city, helping to deal with life's issues and stresses.

Three o'clock came around very quickly and it was time to pick Paul up from school.

Although I could have stayed forever, it was time to go. Michael invited me to come back anytime and suggested I come up for dinner the following night. I graciously accepted, as I knew he knew I would.

My heart was singing as I made my way slowly down the mountain. It felt as though the whole town had been standing still in time while I had been at Michael's, or maybe it was me, just now waking up out of a deep sleep.

Something felt really strange about it all, but oddly very right. Physically I wasn't attracted to him and he was quite a bit older than me. What was it that pulled me to him? I tried to let it go and trusted I would find out soon enough.

The following night couldn't come fast enough for me. I felt enormous anticipation throughout the next day. Finally I got the boys off to bed with only minimal resistance.

I had managed to turn Paul's hysterical bath times into a fun and exciting playtime with bubbles and toys. We hadn't quite achieved the same for bedtime, or not yet anyway. I said goodnight to Mary and Barry who were cuddled up in front of the TV, and I headed back to the mansion on the hill.

What an incredible night. The moon was just beginning to peek through the low-lying cloud, casting its silver light upon the dreamlike landscape.

Again Michael was at the door to greet me but this time with a quick and welcoming kiss. I could see past his shoulder as we embraced. The table was set exquisitely. Candles flickered away as steam rose from the plates, obviously just set out. He must have seen or heard me coming. It was amazing.

I hadn't been treated to this kind of 'romance' in a very long time, in-fact never. I was flattered and a little intimidated.

I had definitely not been brought up with any understanding of the finer things in life. I felt like a hillbilly compared to what Michael had placed before me and I didn't want him to see my ignorance.

Despite my fears, the food was perfect and the wine delightful. Up to this point I was a beer drinker or whatever was available that was cheap and would do the job just as well.

After an hour of sitting on the large leather couch that moulded to hug your body once you sat in it, Michael asked if I would like to sit in the hot-tub, informing me it was kind of a nightly ritual for him. I am a willing participant when it comes to any hot water so I let him lead me out through the dark crisp night to the back of his house.

Out in the open, surrounded by lush palms and ferns, nestled the hot tub. I slid in quickly; a little self-conscious at my nakedness but the moonlight had a way of making everything it touches appear beautiful. The warmth of the water brought chills to my body followed by an amazing sense of comfort.

We spent half an hour talking about our lives and beliefs, listening to the distinguishable call of the morepork owl, and watching the night sky with awe at its vastness and mystery.

Michael moved towards me. Gently touching my face he said he couldn't wait any longer. He pulled me to him and his kiss took me into another world. I felt I was caught up in a dream surely designed for someone else. It was all so hazy, soft, and unreal. My body was then being lifted up by a great force of strength and carried gently into the house while we were still locked in a magical embrace.

It was if we became one. I could feel his heart beating within mine. As we kissed, it was as if we could breathe each other's breath. Everything we needed was right there in that moment. That moment was beyond description. That moment was beyond this world. My mind kept grasping for understanding. The whole experience seemed to be too fixed. It was too easy, too right.   I faded in and out of sensations of pure bliss and passion to confusion and fear. Whatever was happening was powerful and beyond my ability to try to work it out or change it so I relaxed and let go.

I begrudgingly snuck out at around 5am, still immersed in a cloud of ecstasy and emotion.

The sun was just beginning to come up as I gently closed the back door. I hoped not to wake anyone.

Luckily I got to my room, changed clothes and had barely climbed into bed when Paul came running in, jumping on my bed. Barry followed, apologising profusely, claiming the little terror had got away from him. He scalded Paul, stating that from now on he was no longer allowed in my room. They left, closing the door behind them.

The next few days went by very slowly. I wondered if I would see Michael again, why I hadn't heard from him and if I should call him. He resolved my dilemma the following day.

"So did I scare you away?" his voice coming down the phone sounding even sweeter than I remembered.

"I thought I'd wait for you to call. I didn't really know what to make of everything that's happened." I replied.

He assured me that his doors were always open to me and I could come back whenever I wanted.

"How about tonight?" he asked.

"Well, I have a meeting in town tonight, but if you don't mind it being quite late, then I'd love to stop in"

"No problem, see you then" he responded.

I let Mary and Barry know that I might not make it back that night and that I'd have to see how late it gets. They said that was fine and that I didn't need to be back until around lunchtime the following day. Mary gave me a shopping list and Barry asked me to pick up a couple of things he wasn't able to find in the local store before I headed off for the city.

I tried to make these 'full' days in town, giving me plenty of time to stop in and see family and friends.

It turned out to be a wonderful day with a powerful message coming through the channelling that evening.

During the meditation I was shown Michael and I coming from the same place. We use the same energy and not only were we able to breathe each other's breath, our energy forms are totally integrated and connected.

I arrived just after 11:30 to find Michael in the hot tub so I joined him. We continued to spend many more nights together and gradually I began to spend more days there as well. Whenever I could get away from the kids and cleaning, I would retreat to that place of paradise on the hill.

Spiritual experiences were getting more intense and my journeys into the city had become lessons.

Each time I drove there or back I would have a leaning experience. Sometimes it was as simple as my car stopping for no apparent reason.

On one occasion I sat on the side of the road with my car refusing to start. By this time I had learnt enough about trusting these things, and it wasn't long before a gentleman arrived offering to help.

For no apparent reason he began talking about an emotional situation he was in so I responded with words given in the moment. Twenty minutes later he drove off with me assuring him I would be fine there, still unable to start the car. As soon as he had left, the car started right up.

I know I was being taught about listening and trusting.

Another time as I was driving in to the city, I came to some new traffic lights. They were right on the motorway and hadn't been there the previous week. They turned red and it looked like I wasn't going to be able to stop in time. I put my foot on the brakes to slow down but there was nothing there. I realised at that point I had a choice of how I was going to deal with this situation.

The previous month had been full of journeys to and from the city at night where animals or vehicles had appeared out of nowhere on the road in front of me. I felt as though I was being tested for my reactions.

Realising this, I knew I needed to not react with fear in any of these situations. So I didn't. I remained calm, and as a result as I approached the intersection, I felt time slow down. It was as if I had all the time in the world to work out what I was going to do. Luckily I didn't need to. It seemed that the action or decision of 'no-fear' was enough.

As time sped back up to its normal pace, the pressure returned beneath my foot and I stopped within plenty of time.

I felt empowered by this knowledge. Strength entered my life where I had felt so helpless before. I no longer felt as though I needed to fear anything. I was totally protected and guided. I could control the way things happen to me.

One afternoon when I got back from picking Paul up from school, Mary was in tears. She told me she had just come back from the doctors who had told her she was looking at losing the baby. I tried to comfort her and after a cup of tea I asked if she would like me to do some healing on her.

I'm not sure why I asked her that because I had never done a 'healing' before. I had seen it done plenty of times as a young child when my mother would take me to the local spiritual church.   Mary said she would think about it. She was waiting to hear back from one last doctor who might be able to help.

I found the next couple of days difficult. Things had changed and I felt as though Mary and Barry had begun to take advantage of me. They no longer asked or informed me when they were leaving, sometimes for days at a time. They would just leave the kids with me and go. I didn't always even know where they were going. It was starting to go against the agreement we had made in the beginning to do with hours of work and availability.

A few days later on her arrival back from the doctors, Mary asked me for the healing I had offered.

I had her lie down on her bed and I placed my hands above her stomach as I had seen others do. I was nervous and didn't know what to do next so I prayed. I called on my guides, the ascended Masters, the Council of Light and any other Light Beings of pure energy to assist in this healing. I asked that God's Will be done and that if it was meant to be, to let this mother and child be healed.

Within a minute, I felt the most intense shock, or bolt of energy race through my body. I felt as though I had been struck by lightening. Energy poured in through the top of my head and out my hands like a liquid blue light with a strong magnetic pull.

This energy was twisting under my hands, that were about four inches off Mary's stomach, causing them to move in a circular motion above her.

At this point Mary opened her eyes as she could feel it as well. The energy was turning the baby in the womb.

Never before had I experienced anything like it.

The ten minutes we spent seemed like an eternity before the energy in my hands stopped and my arms fell to my sides. There was no need for words, as we both knew it was going to be all right. The top of my head felt bruised but I felt enlivened and very blessed.

I went to my room to do some meditation. I needed to find out what I was going to do as far as the job situation.

As I sat on my bed, I felt an unfamiliar energy build up within me. Intensifying right in front of me where a green light began to appear. It became a ball of light about two feet across and then gradually began to change form. Despite my disbelief, it transformed into the letter 'G' and then 'O'.

Instantly I knew I had to do it. Michael had said I could stay with him if I ever wanted to, so I packed up my few possessions, rounded up the animals, and left.

The timing was actually perfect. I heard a couple of days later that Mary had gone into labour and delivered a premature, but living baby boy.

I guess my purpose had been fulfilled and there was no need to hang around any longer! I wasn't too happy about the way it had to end with bad feelings but I convinced myself it was the way it needed to be for whatever reason. I just had to trust in the whole process.

It was like a breath of fresh air at Michael's. I spent many hours roaming over the hundred and fifty acres he owned, finding waterfalls and caves. I would discover tranquil areas on the land that I had a hard time leaving.

As I sat to soak it all in, I felt the presence of nature spirits. I found myself connecting with the earth in a magical way. The earth became personal to me. It was like I could feel her heartbeat. If I really listened, I could even hear her song.

At the time I didn't question it much as I was so caught up in the moment, just absorbing as much of it as I could. It seemed so natural. I was able to sit with the trees and they would pass on information to me about the past and people who had been in the area. I found they would also pass on information about their medicinal benefits. I would normally receive this information by feeling a part of my body tingle ~ I then knew to use it for that organ etc.

A storm hit one night and Michael was worried about the small kids in the paddock. We hurried to move as many as we could into shelters, but we found two in bad condition. With them liable to catch pneumonia so easily, Michael called his vet to come out immediately. We placed them in a pen, surrounding them with hay and dried them off as best we could.

I was drawn to only one of the kids, so I held its head and asked for healing. I felt the energy flowing from my hands and felt the kid comforted in some way. Despite my wanting to go to the other kid, I felt this one needed me.

The vet arrived and treated the other kid first while Michael and I went back to the house to dry off.

When the vet came up to let us know he was on his way home, he informed us that the kid I had done the healing on had gone. I was shocked. I didn't understand. What had the healing been for? I asked for guidance and later that evening was graced by the presence of Sananda who told me that the other kid was going to survive regardless, but I needed to help the other one as it passed over.

It was a strange emotion I was feeling, and I didn't know how to feel about helping someone or something die. It was a situation I hadn't given much thought to until that moment. I guess to do healing means in whatever way is needed, not necessarily in the way I think it be done or received.

Three months had passed and my relationship with Michael was going perfectly. We had so many things in common and we enjoyed each other's company. I almost felt like a princess in a fairytale world, until that night.

I was woken at around two in the morning with my name being called. I bolted upright in bed, with my eyes struggling to adjust to the darkness. As usual there was no one there.

A light began to slowly appear at the end of the bed and I saw it was Sananda.

I gently pulled back the covers and tiptoed into the living room, closing the door behind me as quietly as I could.

Once embraced by the oversized, cold leather chair, Sananda's face formed again before me.

His familiar voice claimed, "You have to make a choice right now."

"What choice?" I thought.

"You have to decide if you want to have children. If you make this choice, you will stay and have children with Michael."

I was somewhat shocked by the suddenness and seriousness of this request.

"What is the most beneficial for my purpose?" I sent back to him.

"It won't affect the outcome at all. You are free to choose either way. The choice to have children will only influence your alternate path by about five years."

I couldn't believe it. Michael had been talking a lot about having children as he was getting up there in age, and up until this point it had felt right. But now I didn't know. What if this was my only chance to have children?

My mind wandered back nine years to when I was involved with Warren. He was my saviour in a way. My Mother had a male friend move in with us barely days after my Father had left. This man wasn't particularly nice to my younger brother, my mother or me. He would drink quite a lot and then start putting my mother down. I didn't like it so I asked my mother if I could have more time to get to know him before he moved in, but she didn't want to hear what I had to say. I pretty much gave her an ultimatum at that point and she chose to have him in her life instead of me.

I had been seeing Warren for a few months by that time. He was nearly four years older than me, which at fourteen was quite a lot. We met one night outside the local pub. I was selling marijuana and he bought some from me.

I wasn't a drug dealer, just a kid who found some plants on our property, so I was just putting them to use. I needed the money and it was a one-off situation with a very small amount.

Warren was just what I needed at the time. He was handsome, sweet and he was interested in me.

Once my mother informed me of her priorities, I moved in with Warren and his family.

Three generations lived in his house, which wasn't uncommon amongst Maori people, and they were very warm and inviting.

I continued to go to school for the next year, and life was ok.

We lived for the parties and fishing trips in the weekends.

Then one night after a party at our house, Warren snapped. A rage was building inside him as he accused me of flirting with someone at the party.

I tried to assure him that no such thing had happened but he didn't believe me.

Before I knew it I was flying across the room and my head hit the window ledge. It was such a strange sensation, it didn't really even hurt and the whole event was caught up in that state of no-time or suspended time.

I didn't know what to do, so I just lay there, watching this person I didn't know anymore go through some type of emotional process before returning to himself.

At that point he broke down and cried, professing his love for me and that he would never do that again. I felt sorry for him as I could see there was so much pain he was going through. The fleeting thoughts of leaving him transformed. So I stayed.

From that point on it became a regular habit.

I dreaded the parties because I knew what was coming after it. He had hooked me in emotionally so well that I had a hard time leaving.

He became very controlling, not allowing me to contact family, work, or even go to the doctor to get the contraceptive. I therefore became pregnant.

At first I thought it was a good thing because now the beatings would stop and maybe it would help him calm down at the same time. At that time I also wanted desperately for something of my own and thought having a baby was a blessing in disguise.

I told my mother who proceeded to have an emotional fit.

I had never heard her talk that way before

"I will not let you have a black baby!" she cried.

I tried to reason with her but she was adamant.

A visit to the hospital was arranged in secret, as an abortion would never be accepted in a Maori family.

My mother convinced me to pretend I had a miscarriage whereby she would turn up and tell the family she was taking me to the hospital for a check-up.

It worked for the most part, except for my guilt and one of Warren's sisters, who never really believed I had a miscarriage.

The next time I fell pregnant we had moved in to our own place so Warren would have more control over me.

He wouldn't let me leave him and yet he would beat me nearly every week that I was there. I was no longer left on my own. Whenever he went out, he would have one of his friends stay with me to make sure I didn't leave. I was imprisoned.

He would sometimes bring home girls, dragging me in to the bedroom to watch him have sex with them.

He probably thought it would hurt me, but he had no clue as to the despise I felt for him at that time. I cringed at the thought of him touching me, and I would spend hours going through different scenarios to escape that prison.

I came to the point where I saw only two options. One was to kill him and the other was to kill myself. Well, I didn't have it in me to kill anyone and if I killed myself I knew he would hurt my dog, Troy. I felt totally helpless.

Sometimes I would think I could just knock him out and run, but I convinced myself that if I didn't manage to knock him out properly I would get a beating beyond all. My next fear was that if I started to hit him, my pain would come out and I wouldn't be able to stop.

Sex to him was rape to me, and as a result, I became pregnant again. Thinking maybe this time would give him a chance to change, I had hope.
I underestimated his demons.

Initially he was ecstatic, but it soon turned to fear.
He came to me in a fit of rage, claiming that it wouldn't work because the baby would take all my attention away from him. "There's only one thing to do..." he said before lodging several life-threatening fisted blows to my abdomen.

I suffered immensely. Unable to receive doctor's treatment because of Warren's fear of losing control, I was bedridden for about a month, unable to function, partly due to the physical injuries, partly because my spirit had been broken. I only lived at that moment, to protect my dog. Warren knew it too, and would threaten to hurt Troy if I didn't do what he asked.

Eventually Warren realised he had to get help when I couldn't stop vomiting.

Four days had passed of this and I had got to the point where my stomach lining was coming out.

I didn't have the strength to leave the house so he called a doctor in who quickly gave me a shot of something to prevent the reaching. He then gave me plenty of glucose water to help re-hydrate my body. He didn't prescribe drugs or do much other than tell me I should learn meditation or some form of relaxation as the vomiting was stress related.

I couldn't tell him about my situation with Warren standing over me and after all, I had tried that with the police and paid the price.

We had been walking home one night and Warren was already enraged thinking one of his friends had been coming on to me. He knocked me to the ground and kicked me a couple of times when a police car pulled up.

"What's going on here?" One of the officers asked.

"Oh nothing, she's drunk, you know. Have to keep her in line" Warren told them.

They agreed with him and drove off telling him to keep it off the street.

I had pleaded with them to lock me up if they wouldn't lock him up, but they didn't care. Needless to say, the repercussions ensured and I never did that again.

A couple of years passed like that. At times Warren sought me out with knives and other sharp objects. Another time he beat me to the ground, continuing to kick me while a group of people looked on. They all knew him and would never stand up to him.

On one occasion however, a man did step in claiming Warren was going to kill me if he kept it up.

I heard Warren through the blood now beginning to dry in my ears and the haze in my head say, "I know, I want to kill her!"

I eventually managed to get out of that relationship, scarred, but alive and a whole lot wiser.

Strangely I have no ill feelings towards him either.

Once out of it I realised he was terrified. He felt that the only way he could keep me in his life was by forcing me to stay. He thought so little of himself that no one would possibly want to be with him. So in a sense, he did do it out of Love.

It wasn't right, but I understood it, and can have compassion for him.

It must be an awful place to be emotionally. Now I don't hesitate to help when I see someone being forced or hit. That relationship taught me a lot and certainly set me up for my path. I also realised that I could let the experience mess up the rest of my life or I could learn and grow from it; becoming a better person. I believe I have become a better person for it.

"No. I would have to say no." I said as I became aware again of the room around me.

I felt sure and clear that I had made the right choice.

Surrounding me with energy of Love and Support, Sananda replied, "Very well, you must leave right away."

I wasn't sure exactly what he meant, but he clarified by telling me I needed to move out straight away. If I was not going to have children with Michael, I needed to leave him.

I was blown away at the seeming absurdity of it. Unable to sleep, I made a cup of tea and sat out on the deck looking out over the mystical land I had thought would be my home for a long time to come and knew this would be the last time I would see this view.

5   LEAP OF FAITH

"I have to go." I told Marshall the following morning.

He was shocked and confused.

I explained as best I could but knew he didn't, and couldn't possibly understand.

I understood he was destined to have children, in fact it was important for him to, and if I wasn't going to provide them for him, I needed to be out of the picture so someone else could.

I didn't know where to go, but settled on a camping ground at a beach not too far away.

When I walked into the camp office that morning to see what sort of opportunities would be available it was like walking right back into a dream I had had a couple of nights ago. The owners were exactly as the dream had revealed and the little pony being led by a young girl confirmed to me the incredible way the universe provides clues and signposts for us along the way just to let us know we're on the right track.

I felt blessed to be there at that moment. It was perfect.

Not surprisingly they needed an extra hand around the camp and I was provided with a caravan in return for a couple of hours work a week. There were only a few people coming through the camp at this time of year so it was very peaceful.

Even the mighty roar of the ocean was calming.

I spent a lot of time on the beach, riding the camp horse, and meditating.

I had begun to see lights in the sky just off the coastline and had felt drawn a couple of times to 'tune-in' to the source of them.

I guess I had always believed in UFO's, I'm not sure if it was something my mother introduced to me or not. I do remember her telling me about a time when I was one or two.

She was walking me in the pram up the road we lived on when she noticed a strange silence. No sounds of neighbourhood children laughing and crying, cars starting up to head back to work after a quick lunch break, and most noticeable was the absence of the sounds of nature; not one bird chirping. Nothing moved. Everything but she and I, had been frozen in time.

Something compelled her to look up to where she saw a shinning silver disk dart through low hanging clouds. That was all she could recall from the experience although she was aware time had vanished, as she was unable account for a couple of hours.

What I was seeing weren't silver disks, they were an amazing display of lights flicking between vibrant primary colours, intermingled with the odd pastel. They moved in strange patterns and I could normally feel their presence before seeing them.

I wanted to find out what or who they were, so I sent out many thoughts for them to communicate to me.

It was a quiet cold day. The driving rain was heavy enough to carve out small pathways in the loose metal driveways. It was far too dreary to get out in it so I sat in my wee caravan occupying my time by catching up on some reading I had been meaning to do for quite awhile.

At dinner time I went over to the communal kitchen room and prepared a small dinner. Taking it into the TV room to eat, I settled into the only comfortable chair in the room and turned on the TV… static. No picture or noise, just static.

I fiddled with the aerial and checked all the channels with no luck.

As I sat back down to eat my dinner I was overwhelmed with a 'knowing' or 'desire' to go back to the caravan and meditate. I followed my intuition as always, and as soon as I sat on my bed I felt myself going into a very deep state of meditation.

I had no idea what had transpired when I came-to, twenty minutes later. I knew I had been in contact with someone, but I had no idea what it was about.

I felt myself coming back to my body and a voice telling me, "You can go back to your program now."

I sat for a few minutes to get my bearings before heading back to the TV room. Sure enough the TV was fine. In that moment, I realised how easily manipulated things can be in this life… If only I could learn how to access it.

I certainly trusted more in 'fate' or 'destiny' because of these experiences.

About a month later after talking to Jenny about all my experiences at the campground, she organised a trip up to stay for a weekend with her family. Roy could do some fishing and she and I could do some direct work with these 'beings'.

Jenny had vivid memories of being taken aboard a 'vessel' or 'craft' when she was younger so felt a strong desire to find out as much as she could about them.

The whole family arrived the following Saturday, put up the tent and had barely set up the camping gear before Roy disappeared with rod and buckets.

Jenny, the kids and I walked along the beach, playing in the surf, and then headed back to the camp to ride on the horse.

Through our many discussions about our lives so far, Jenny and I had discovered that we had come extremely close to meeting each other as children. I loved horses.

Never having one of my own, I went to a pony club in the weekends to ride. I spent quite a bit of time at my Grandmother

and Aunt's house, which was right next to a large grazing area. I would often wander across to it, patting and feeding the horses the 'greener' grass on my side of the fence.

Jenny, I had discovered, kept her horse in the very same paddock at that same time, and her Grandmother had lived right across the street from mine.

Roy wandered back a few hours later with a couple of nice snapper that he cleaned and prepared for dinner.

A quarter-moon was coming up, providing a soft glow across the ocean for us to admire as we ate dinner on the beach.

With the kids tucked in bed and Roy happily reading his latest fantasy novel, Jenny and I headed up the mountain, past Michael's house to sit and see if we could get any type of communication going with our planetary brothers.

We found a perfect place to park the car. It was quite chilly but we braved it, putting on another layer of clothes and climbing onto the hood of my little car.

We spotted the 'craft' off in the western sky so began our 'tuning-in'. Ultimately we sent thoughts out that if they are of the light we would like to have some communication with them.

We waited for hours… nothing.

Again we put thoughts out that we would leave if nothing happened pretty quickly, yet nothing came.

Feeling let down and perhaps a little crazy, we decided it just wasn't meant to be.

As we got back in to the car, we saw a ball of flashing light come strait towards us at unbelievable speed. Before it reached the car however, it vanished.

Seconds passed as we tried to make sense of it, and then I was urged to drive. I could feel this 'craft' above the car so I started the car up and drove back down the hill towards the camp.

Halfway down the road we were amazed to see a rainbow across the road. A rainbow at 11 or 12 o'clock at night was weird but this one also had a white light dome underneath it.

I slowed to a stop right before it, not sure what to do. It felt right to carry on so we entered the energy under the rainbow.

We felt a wave of energy encompass us. It wasn't an uncomfortable feeling but we knew we were in the presence of something very powerful.

Moving out the other side of the rainbow/dome, we knew something had happened to us that our consciousnesses wouldn't be able to grasp.

Before we had time to talk or even think about what we had just experienced, the 'rainbow' flew from above us, disappearing down the hill and appeared to land in a field at the bottom of the mountain. I tried to find a way to get down to it but all the roads led away from the clearing. Exhausting our options we figured we had seen what we needed to, so headed back to the camp.

As we drove along the estuary the object appeared again, this time following us. I pulled over to the side of the road while we watched it dart around in amazing patterns. It then changed direction, heading north and disappeared into a vortex as if it had gone into warp drive.

This action seemed to have the most impact on us. Not only was it the most beautiful thing to see, but we knew it was trying to show us something. I felt as though they were showing us the doorway into other dimensions. A gateway.

Jenny and I sat for a few moments discussing what we had seen; just to make sure either one of us weren't seeing things that weren't really there.

Tired yet exhilarated, we crept back in to the camp and tried to sleep.

The rest of the weekend was uneventful. We knew whoever they were wanted us to believe, and we knew we had been shown something very special.

Life on the beach was as close to paradise as you could get. The mornings were spent cleaning cabins used the night before, and then the rest of the day was mine.

Endless white-sand beach, horses at my disposal and ultimate weather. I had 'stumbled' upon a lifestyle I could get very comfortable with.

Meditations had become powerful with beings of light gracing me with their presence nightly and I became aware of my connections to the Ashtar Command and the whole 'Sirius' and 'Pleaidean' energy.

The messages I was receiving were now corresponding to the lights in the sky and I knew the 'vessels' I had been seeing belonged to the pleaidean's.

Communications with them in meditation revealed their purpose to help the planet in its process of rising of consciousness.

I focused on allowing myself to receive as much energy and information from these beings as I could; knowing that I had something to do with this process, I just couldn't remember what.

I began to feel it was time to move again. These sensations were becoming familiar to me now and I didn't resist or question them as I had in the past. I had faith that I was being guided on my path, and if I trusted in my heart; instead of analysing or putting any sort of logic to it, I would be led on the path of least resistance.

These sensations would start out with a feeling of completion and a strong desire to move on, eventually becoming so strong I would just have to go.

I was learning that because of my purpose here, I would have to move around a lot and I was more than aware I was unable to see the full picture of that purpose and plan, therefore I wouldn't always understand why I had to do certain things.

I just had to trust in this great unseen force, and my connection to it.

So again I set off. 'North' was as much guidance as I got.

I followed back-roads through rugged countryside, spending two nights sleeping in the front seat of my car.

As before, I was shown a face, during a vision, I knew would have something to do with my next step.

It was getting late in the afternoon and I had been driving all day when I came upon a small beachside town.

I had arrived.

I could feel immediately it was right. I was glad it was here, still on the east coast, which I loved, and not that much further north than the camp I had spent the last few months at.

The previous two days had been spent driving right across to the west coast and back. It definitely was a beautiful country.

This part of the coast felt 'light', as if it held a higher vibration than other areas.

So here I was in Mangawhai.

For the city folk it served as a small, fun, holiday destination. The weather is always reasonably moderate and summertime is perfect.

I drove down to the main beach area and hiked up a cliff above it.

At the very top, right on the edge was an area of soft, bright green, lush grass. It was just the perfect dimensions and softness for my tent.

Within a few trips I had hauled up all my camping goods, set the tent up, and settled in before the sun began to go down.

I spent two weeks up there, not coming down at all. In a sense it was like a 'vision quest'.

I watched my environment change many times a day, from deep greys within the ocean and skies to brilliant blues and emerald greens. The ocean showed how alive it really was.

I watched people on the beach below me, totally oblivious to my presence. A new taste of peace began to emerge within me.

I was cooking my breakfast on a small camp burner stove one morning when I noticed a blade of grass. I knew it was a normal blade of grass but I was seeing it in a completely new way. It was one of the most beautiful things I had ever seen.

The reality of its creation overwhelmed me and brought tears to my eyes. I felt like a new person; awakened to a new sense of 'being'.

Placing my legs over the edge of the cliff, I sat, totally absorbed in my surroundings, connecting with nature.

I spotted two dolphins swimming close to the shore. They continued on their journey south until they were directly in front of me, stopping to jump out of the water. They began somersaulting and dancing within the waves.

My hands began to heat up with a slight tingle and then were drawn up until they extended towards the frolicking dolphins. Intense heat beamed from the centre of my palms, going directly towards the dolphins.

I was aware of some communication going on but my mind couldn't comprehend it. It was a beautiful exchange of Love, leaving me feeling exceptionally blessed.

The burning heat from my hands subsided after about ten minutes with my arms falling back to my sides as they did at the completion of healings, and the dolphins continued along their original path.

Still on a high from that experience I headed down to my car for the first time in two weeks.

A note had been placed on my windshield from the local police asking me to contact them as soon as possible.

Thinking there was an emergency I raced to the local police office.

Apparently, they had noticed my car sitting in the car park for a while and had become concerned. My family had been called and search parties had been sent out around the rocks, thinking I had been washed off while fishing.

Stories had also spread through town that I was having an affair with one of the farmers around the coast a bit. I laughed it up the hill to where I was.

I called my family who were preparing to make a trip up, thinking the worst had happened.

My father told me he knew I was OK and said he would feel it if something had happened to me.

I then went to the local store to stock up on food.

Coming out of the store I saw the face that was in my dream a couple of weeks ago; white hair, fair skin, and goatee. He even resembled a goat in a strange way.

I found it too awkward to approach him so I walked past, stopping at the notice board to avoid eye contact. The local pub was advertising a great band that night. I decided it would be good for me at this point to have some human contact, so I would go.

I arrived at around ten o'clock and the band had already been playing for a couple of hours with everyone having a great time.

There he was again, my goat-man, in the corner with a group of friends.

In my heart I knew he would be there, I felt the timing was right. I could feel him watching me for about half an hour before he walked over, introducing himself as Peter.

We had a wonderful conversation that turned philosophical very quickly and as the band wound up for the evening, he asked me if I'd like to carry on the conversation at his place.

We talked until the very wee hours of the morning. He was fascinated by spirituality, asking many insightful questions and sharing experiences he had had.

When he discovered where I was staying, he offered me his spare bed, claiming a storm was on the way.

"And how would you know that?" I asked him.

He told me about his passion for surfing and he always knew what the weather was up to; "…it's vital to a hard-core surfer."

After a couple of hours sleep, I made my way back to my tent, packed up all my gear, sent out thanks to the universe for the wonderful time I had had on this mountain top, and moved in to Peter's little cottage.

The following months went by very quickly. Peter and I formed a wonderful relationship, travelling around the area to some magical places whenever the surf was right.

I started running some 'spiritual development' classes at the local community centre as I found there were a lot of people in the area who were interested in learning about their spirituality but didn't know how to go about it.

A regular group of ten to twenty gathered every week and I would bring in guest speakers who would add insight and understanding about all things relevant to spirit.

I didn't need a lot of money to survive but I was still travelling in to the city every week so I needed gas money.

Sometimes I would receive donations from healings in the form of money, other times organic vegetables. I would buy a lotto ticket whenever I could, and without fail, whenever I was short and needed gas or food, I would win a small amount to get me by.

I loved this way of living. It was scary in a way, but ultimately; when I let go, it always worked out.

I always had what I needed, when I needed it.

Peter had chronic asthma and used his inhaler up to three times a day, so I asked him if he'd like for me to do some healing on him, which he jumped at. He was however, going to be away that night staying in a town further north where he worked at a surf shop.

I assured him it would be fine as I could do a 'distant healing' and he could help by lying down and relaxing at ten o'clock that evening when I would 'tune-in' for the healing.

At ten o'clock while in meditation I was instantly drawn in to a healing chamber. I saw Peter lying on a table and there were several light-beings standing around him. I had learnt that there would normally be others present during a healing, sometimes the person's guide, other times ascended masters, angels or deceased family members.

On this occasion one of these beings approached me, telling me that he had created a device to help Peter really relax during the healing; enabling the work to be done on a deep level.

He showed me what appeared to be goggles and stated that since Peter was such a Star Trek fan, he would be able to watch a new series through them as we worked on him.

This Being exuded enormous pride and love as he placed the goggles upon Peter, and we began the healing.

My hands were taken through Peter's body and I felt a dark, sticky residue clinging on to his bones and within his blood system.

Above his stomach was a gel-like substance that I pulled up and out of him. In spaghetti-like cords, I could feel it peeling away, releasing its hold on ligaments, tissue, bone, and finally out of his blood; massive amounts that didn't seem to want to stop.

I continued for nearly an hour before it ceased, at which time I was brought out of the meditation.

The following evening when Peter arrived home from work he told me how wonderful he felt and hadn't needed to use his inhaler once.

I described to him what I had experienced but he was more concerned with the possibility of a new Star Trek series than the details of the healing session.

I began to draw again; something I hadn't done in a very long time.

I typically used pencil and had been commissioned by a local real-estate agent to draw some houses they had going on to the real estate market.

Between this and the healing donations, I was able to pay rent and survive comfortably.

On one particular evening I made my way to the city for my usual Thursday night channelling at Lisa's, feeling uneasy.

I had arranged to stay over at Dad's that night to save the drive back so late at night, but something wasn't sitting right with me. When I arrived home the following day, I could feel the presence of another woman in the batch and knew Peter had been unfaithful.

I waited for him to get home from work, thinking he would talk to me about what happened, but he didn't say a word.

I was taken out to an expensive meal and given flowers; a gesture of his guilt I'm sure.

Right before he had every intention of making love to me, I told him I knew what he had done. He was stunned but couldn't deny it.

It was time for me to move on. I put energy out requesting guidance for my next move.

The following day when I went to the beach to collect some driftwood for a carving I was being inspired to do, I found a couple of different pieces of unique wood and began whittling away with a kitchen knife.

Allowing my inner guidance to lead, at the end of the day I had what looked like a short staff of some sort. I had inlayed some of the darker, denser wood in patterns around it and the shape at the bottom looked like a crystal.

Holding it and asking for clarity, I was given that it was infused with a crystalline energy; not needing the real thing, just the essence, and it would be as effective as any powerful crystal.

The rest of the dark wood was carved into an image of Mother Mary.

Peter was staying at his job overnight so I got to bed early. I had amazing dreams with many adventures and visions. A light in the room woke me in the middle of the night and I saw what looked like a thin beam of blue light coming in through the window and landing on the head of the Mother Mary carving I had placed on my bedside table. Dazed from waking out of such a deep sleep I effortlessly drifted back into my previous dreams.

The first thing I noticed when I woke the next morning was Mary staring right at me.

When I had placed her on the bedside table the previous night, she was facing the window. I suddenly remembered the light during the night and I began to gather my senses pretty quickly.

I looked around the room and noticed that all my candles had melted. Most of them had never been used but they now lay twisted and contorted by what looked like a lot of heat.

I had no idea what had happened during the night but I was beginning to sense urgency. For what, I didn't know.

The entire day was consumed with a 'leaving' feeling. I had felt this many times before but this felt bigger, stronger and somehow more important than the others.

As I got into my car for my usual journey to Lisa's meeting, I asked my guides for confirmation or some sort of clarity of my feelings.

By the time I reached the city, I realised I had been singing a song the entire trip. It was 'I'm leaving on a jet plane'.

I took this as my confirmation and thanked my helpers. Something would now have to show up to allow that to happen.

The next day I pulled out my drawing paper and thumbing through some old copies of the National Geographic, I was drawn to an image of a Native American Indian. I was compelled to draw him but was not very willing.

I had never been able to draw faces well, in that my interpreted proportions always left them looking very 'Picaso'd'.

Despite my fears, I gave it a go and was amazed when it came together reasonably easily.

As I drew, I began to feel a presence behind me and by 'tuning in' to its energy, realised it was the spirit of the man I was drawing.

I was amazed at the contrast in what I was experiencing. The photo was stern and threatening, but the personality now next to me was humorous and light.

I drew a few Indian images that day with all appropriate spirits present.

What was it about this culture that was now pulling me in? I knew nothing about the Indians of America.

During a meditation that night my guide informed me that I in fact had a mission to complete with the Indians. Initially I went into denial.

I had worked in the hospitality industry for years and the only Americans I had met were obnoxious and fake. America was the last place on earth I wanted to go, and I didn't even want to leave New Zealand. Actually I had never even considered leaving New Zealand until that moment; it was my home and it was perfect.

I resolved the issue by stating to the Universe, "If I'm meant to go, then let it be. I'm staying out of it so you make it happen."

I had no money, no passport and no idea where I would even go. My beloved helpers must have gone into overtime, because within a week I had money, passport, visas, airline ticket and direction to visit the Hopi Indians in Northern Arizona.

Things had fallen into place so sweetly I couldn't deny it any longer.

It was like a dream, with me remaining neutral. The details and connections came to me effortlessly. I met a lady through my Father who told me about the Hopis. She gave me the name of her friend in Flagstaff, saying he might be able to take me out to the reservation. My Father bought my car from me so I would have the cash for my ticket, and my mother's paperwork came through smoothly from England, allowing me 'Right of Abode' there.

I was to fly to L.A., stay three months, then head to England to visit my mother. That's where my ticket ended.

My Father took me to a clairvoyant in Tauranga for a reading with a lady who had come highly recommended.

By this time I considered my healing and spiritual work to be my career, and the Command or 'White Brotherhood' Masters, to be my employers.

I was amused when this clairvoyant told me that my 'job' was sending me overseas and for me not to worry as my 'employers' were taking care of all the details like accommodation and transport; which was just another little message for me to totally trust in the 'Divine' plan.

I was definitely a believer at this point; I was being given every opportunity to trust in a greater power and purpose.

A strong 'warrior' feeling was stirring within me and I knew I was about to go on an adventure of a lifetime. I had committed my life to my spiritual purpose; not thinking or wanting anything for my own 'personality' aspect, and now I was finally getting to live it. I can't begin to describe what I was feeling.

I was aware of constantly fighting my mind, which wanted to convince me what I was doing was 'insane' and everyone else would be thinking the same thing.

"She's really crazy! She hears voices telling her to go to America, what a weirdo!"

These thoughts raced around my mind, intermingled with a tremendous fear of flying. It was too much to handle and a couple of nights before I was due to leave I fell out of my bed, dizzy and nauseous.

There was no way I was going to be able to get on a plane in that condition. I wouldn't be able to go.

I however knew that wasn't an option, so I called a friend who practiced kinesiology, asking if he thought he could help. After one session that day, I went to bed the same night excited about my impending flight.

It seemed absolutely everything had fallen into its right place, even my fears. Nothing left but to get on the plane and head off to another world.

I wasn't sure if I would even be coming back to New Zealand. It was exciting and scary, but incredibly invigorating. My whole Soul was enlivened as my pathway unfolded before me.

I set my tent up in the back yard to make sure there were no holes and that the zips worked ok.

I had just got it set up when there was a huge object that landed on the side. I jumped out of the tent in a hurry to find my cat Cling-on recovering from his rebound. He then surprised me by running towards the tent and jumping at the side of it again.

He was using it like a trampoline. It was hilarious but he was putting claw holes in it so I packed it up quickly, much to his obvious disgust.

I wondered what kinds of places I would end up using this tent in. I was almost too excited to sleep that night but I knew it would be a long tiring flight so I used some meditation techniques to relax.

The alarm woke me at 4:30am and I quietly moved about the kitchen preparing a cup of tea and some toast.

Sarah was picking me up to take me to the Sunday Markets. We wanted to get there really early before most of the real bargains disappeared, even if we had to use a flashlight to see them.

I finished my breakfast and went outside to wait at the top of the driveway.

It was a beautiful, crisp morning.

I sat on the cold cement of the driveway looking at the sky, which was clear, filled with many stars despite the city lights.

A peace seemed to come over me and I felt relaxed for the first time in at least four days. My mind wasn't racing so I took in my surroundings, really seeing them as if I may never again.

I then saw a huge ball of blue light move directly over the city from what looked like east to west. I had no idea what it was that I had just seen, but my attention was quickly distracted with Sarah's car pulling up.

The market was busy, even at the insanely early hour we got there; bargain hunters galore.

We slowly wandered around. I wasn't looking for anything as my backpack was full to the brim, but it was interesting to see what was there and it was my last chance to spend some time with Sarah.

At a small stall off to the side of the main area, a man called me over and told me I needed to have a piece of greenstone he had. It was a lovely piece but it was big.

Greenstone is extremely heavy. It had a base of greenstone as well, and was about six inches high. No way could I cart something like that around the world in my backpack.

"Only $165" he said.

I politely told him I wasn't interested and carried on to the next stall.

On our second time around the market, the same man called me over again.

"I'll let you have it for $50" he said this time.

That was a good price but apart from not having the room, I didn't have the money.

A couple of hours later, after we had stopped at a coffee shop to rest our feet, we headed back to the car taking a shortcut through a side street.

This path took us straight past the stall with the man and the greenstone. This time he wouldn't let me leave without it. "You have to have it," he said, and "I don't know why, but you can have it for $10"

At that, I paid him the $10 and took the greenstone graciously. Despite my wanting to leave it with someone in New Zealand, I knew it had to make the journey with me.

6   THE LAND OF OPPORTUNITIES

I had chosen to fly at night, thinking that if I couldn't see the ground it would make the whole flying experience easier, and maybe if I could sleep through it all I wouldn't even notice I was 30,000 feet up in the air.

My family all turned up at the airport to see me off and we had a nice couple of hours.

My father gave me a hard time when he saw the small plane I was travelling on. Fortunately I was only going as far as Western Samoa on that one, and then I would transfer on to a large plane for the remainder of the trip.

It was an emotional departure, none of us knew how long I would be gone or what would happen. Walking through the gates was a very hard thing for me to do but once I got on the plane I was filled with a 'peace' and 'warrior' energy.

I felt exuberantly liberated and free.

It took me a little while to get used to the flying, but settled quite comfortably in once we were at cruising altitude and surprisingly, enjoyed the journey.

The plane was, for the most part full, but the seats next to me were empty allowing me plenty of room to spread out.

Once in the air, I became aware of a spirit present with me. I tuned in to recognise Jerry.

Jerry was a friend who had died a couple of years prior in a car accident. He was excited for me and just wanted to sit with me for a while. It was nice to have him there with me. I missed him sometimes.

He was a friend of my older brother and despite the efforts of my brother, Jerry and I had had a relationship for a couple of years on and off. It was very casual but we both really enjoyed each other's company. Near the end, he had got into some trouble with the police and had disappeared into the bush. No one really knew where he was, but years later he had told a few people he was coming out to give himself up as he was ready to face the consequences of his actions. On the drive to the police station, he had a 'freak accident'. Killed driving at 30kph.

I felt that the time he spent alone in the bush had allowed him to deal with some pretty heavy issues and in doing so, had fulfilled his life's purpose.

As he began to leave me there in the plane I thanked him for the visit while my thoughts continued to reflect on parts of my life and experiences that had brought me to this point.

I knew my whole experience with Warren had taught me forgiveness and compassion. I knew I couldn't judge people and that there was a reason why I had to go through that entire trauma. It had made me stronger and I don't think I would be sitting on the plane if it hadn't happened. I believe I took the positive from it and now had something to give and share from that whole experience.

At around one o'clock in the morning we made our decent into Western Samoa. It was rough but I had never really flown before so I wasn't sure what to expect.

I felt the plane swaying from side to side and at one point I thought the wings would hit the ground or we would flip over. I then felt as though the pilot was trying to pull up but we were caught in some sort of air pocket. The people on the plane became very silent.

The cabin filled with tension and in that moment I knew something wasn't right. For what seemed like a very long time we struggled with the turbulence but eventually touched down safely. Everybody exploded into applause and then silent prayers of thanks.

With the first leg down it was only twelve hours to go to touch down in Los Angeles.

The wait in Western Samoa was torturous. I was tired and it was so humid I felt as though I wasn't able to get a proper breath. The airport didn't have enough seats and the floor was definitely not a place you'd want to sit. I chose to lean up against the outside wall for the hour it took to transfer luggage over to the 747.

The larger plane was much more comfortable and again I had both seats next to me vacant so this time I could lie down across them and get some good sleep, which I did right after dinner.

I was woken by a presence standing next to me. I opened my eyes to see the spirit of a Hawaiian 'Kahuna'.

He was beautifully dressed in a colourful outfit and had a gentle yet powerful energy.

"I would like to welcome you to my land." He said as he sprinkled me with a white powder that looked like salt, however I was aware it had the most amazing fragrance.

He then left as quietly and as quickly as he had appeared. 'Blessed' hardly described how I felt about his appearance to me. I felt he was honouring my presence there.

At that moment the captain announced that we would be descending into Hawaii and for us to put our seatbelts on.

The visit to Hawaii was brief and my only experience of it was the windowless guarded room we were all shuffled into to wait for re-boarding.

I was really excited when we touched down in LA.

Coming in to land, I saw the flat, palm tree-laden landscape I had only previously seen in the movies. It was so much bigger than I had imagined but certainly lived up to the 'smog city' name it was known for. The subtle yellow haze smothered it, yet in a bizarre way felt like it belonged there.

I breezed through customs and immigration which was surprising because a few people had told me I would be lucky to get in as I had no firm plans or schedules.

I contacted the hotel I was staying at to come and pick me up, then sat and waited.

At one point during my wait a young guy came up and grabbed my pack then started running towards a door. I ran after him, finally catching him and taking my bag back.

He was working for a hostel in the area and claimed it's the way they do things there. I wasn't amused. It was a really strange way to drum up business. I sat back down but held on to my bags a little tighter.

My ride turned up half an hour later and another half an hour vanished before I arrived at the Hotel on Venice Beach.

It was around 8pm and I was very tired from the entire sitting around waiting.

I met Nigel, the Manager, whom my Brother had told me about.

Nigel had some spiritual interests so we hit it off straight away. He showed me to my hostel room where I met my roommate with small-talk then collapsed into bed completely exhausted.

The moment I began to drift off to sleep I felt the bed start shaking furiously. I knew it was an earthquake when I heard sirens outside but I was so tired I didn't care. Unable to retain any form of consciousness, I drifted off to the sounds of chaos outside.

The following morning I felt refreshed and eager to see this famous city. I hadn't really taken any of it in when I arrived last night but as I stepped out the front door I saw the beach a couple of hundred metres away and a whole different smell. It was fascinating.

Nigel came out with a coffee in hand asking me how I slept. I mentioned the earthquake and he assured me it wasn't a major one.

Nigel had Italian blood so had dark hair and complexion, not tall but not too short. He was keen to talk to me about spiritual things and I was keen to get out on to the beach so I asked if he wanted to come for a walk.

"I have to stay close because I'm on duty, but if you like we'll go up top and talk and I'll show you what a big earthquake does."

I had no idea what 'up top' was but I agreed. Nigel made me a cup of coffee and we headed up the five floors to the roof.

For the most part the roof was flat, although in some places it was disappearing into the level below.

"These were some of the after effects of earthquakes" Nigel said.

Despite my obvious discomfort at standing on something that looked like it was waiting for this moment to crumble beneath me, we pulled up a couple of chairs to get a good view out along Venice Beach.

It was a beautiful sunny day and already there were a lot of people out and about. Walkers, runners, roller-bladers and cyclists were all out exercising on the path in front of the hotel.

The sun had not long risen and there was a huge machine, like a grader, going up the beach. Nigel explained that twice a day this machine would work at sifting through the sand to pull up any dirty needles or glass ~ a beach sweeper.

The thought of this was shocking to me and seemed so far from the reality I had lived in.

We talked for a couple of hours, first with Nigel giving me a run-down on the area, hints of places to visit and things to avoid and then we talked spiritual.

He didn't get to talk to many people about things he felt or experienced, so to have someone else understand and even experience the same things was a special treat for him.

A call from the office sequestered Nigel so I decided to head for the beach to have a look around.

Once outside I turned left onto the boardwalk. It was a major culture shock.

There were people everywhere. The boardwalk was lined with shops, stalls and restaurants where people mingled.

Further along on the boardwalk I saw small stalls and groups of people performing a variety of arts. Some were singing, others dancing, some creating amazing paintings with spray cans, there was even a guy juggling chainsaws.

The atmosphere was buzzing with what seemed to be a huge cross-section of people.

I saw street people ranting, business people still talking business on their cell phones while speed walking in Speedos, people wandering around in bikinis and shorts, dogs with sunglasses and hats on. I saw snakes and exotic birds draped over their owners, but the thing that really shocked me was seeing a couple of police officers with guns on their hips.

When you haven't been brought up seeing guns, on one hand it doesn't seem real and on the other it doesn't feel right.

I approached the officers with ease, telling them where I was from and that I wanted to get out to Arizona and had thought of hitchhiking to get there. They were horrified I would even consider hitchhiking. One reason being it was illegal and the other that it was very dangerous. They proceeded to tell me of the last hitchhiker they had picked up off the road, in pieces.

They convinced me to catch a surer and much safer train ride.

They were very friendly and helpful, and eventually began giving me a rundown on some of the people walking past, including the weapons they carried.

Many of these people were known to them and they kept an eye on them because of the trouble they caused regularly.

I spent the next couple of days mainly down on the boardwalk. It was fascinating to sit and watch.

Nigel and I spent quite a bit of time together, talking and eating at some very nice restaurants in the area.

Up to this point the only time I ever went out to a restaurant was on a family member's birthday or some other special occasion; here it was an everyday occurrence.

I learnt all about coffee one day. Not knowing what all the different types of coffee were, I ordered the first on the list.

I got a very small shot-glass of some sort of syrup. Thinking there was more to come; I found a seat and waited. When nothing came and I had tasted the nasty bitter substance, I went back to the counter thinking they had become too busy and forgotten the rest of my order.

I was horrified when I found out I was supposed to drink that syrup as is and that it had cost $3. I left it sitting on the table and vowed never to have another espresso.

The time came to leave for Flagstaff on the train called the 'South-Western Chief'. It had a colourful picture of an Indian chief painted on it which I thought was quite appropriate.

Nigel had driven me to the train station and asked me to keep in touch with him.

As I was boarding the train he handed me a necklace. It was a small green heart made of a semi-precious stone and in that moment I realised he wanted more from me than I was able to give him. I thanked and hugged him, letting him know I would write, and then climbed aboard to continue my journey.

I really enjoyed the train journey. Although the trip was through the night and I wouldn't see much of the landscape, I was assured by a number of people it wouldn't matter as there wasn't much to see and sleep was more important.

Not far out of Los Angeles I was alerted to the presence of yet another spirit with me. This time it was a young Indian warrior, or runner. He informed me that he was to stay with me for the entire journey to ensure my safe arrival.

My purpose here must be important I thought, to be protected. I wasn't sure how to feel about that.

Life had taught me that I didn't matter, that I was no one special. Now it seemed someone was waiting for me and wanted to ensure I got there safely, but whom?

For the rest of the trip I felt this runner's quiet, dedicated presence in the empty seat next to me, and the eerie sense of eyes watching.

It was still dark outside when I opened my eyes. I didn't have a watch so I had no idea what the time was or where I was, all I could make out were faint shapes on the landscape that looked like pyramids.

As the sun began to rise over the next hour, the desert landscape became clearer. I began to feel very comfortable here; as if it was familiar to me despite having never seen anything like it before.

We pulled in to Flagstaff around 5:30 in the morning, much too early to call Anthony.

After organising to leave my luggage at the train station while I looked around the town, I headed out inquisitively into the brisk spring air. Luckily the station was right in the middle of town so I wouldn't have too far to go.

My first impression was that I had gone back in time to a small western town and it wouldn't have shocked me in the slightest to see horses on the road pulling carts. Pubs here were still called saloons and I noticed a couple of stores I could buy a gun from.

Finding nothing open however, I crossed back over the train tracks and went into a hostel.

DeBeau Hostel appeared to be rundown, but I had never stayed in a real hostel before so I was curious enough to give it a go. It was the right price and even supplied breakfast.

I was shown to my dorm room and asked to not make too much noise as the others were still sleeping. I decided to leave my bags at the train station until a reasonable hour.

The young German guy, who checked me in to the hostel gave me rough directions to get around town and told me about a great coffee shop just around the corner. As it was still only 6:30am I headed off to Macey's Coffeehouse, as he had said, it was just around the corner from the hostel.

Macey's was every bit as good as he had described. Upon opening the door you are greeted with the enticing smell of freshly baked bread. The coffee was freshly roasted and ground right there.

I have no doubt the heavenly aroma could call any dormant caffeine addiction out of remission.

My first bagel experience was not disappointing and despite being once bitten, I was prepared to give the whole coffee experience another go. This time I asked for a recommendation for a virgin coffee drinker, which produced a 'Macey's special'.

This was a deliciously rich combination of coffee and chocolate that I knew would get me in to some serious addictive trouble.

The coffeehouse was cosily warm and the aromas from the kitchen provided a sense of comfort, so I decided to give the cool air outside a miss and instead sit and watch people come and go.

It was a friendly atmosphere with most people knowing each other. There was also a 'hippy' feel to it with plenty of dreadlocks I had previously only seen on staunch Rastafarians and I'm sure I even spotted a guy wearing a skirt.

I liked the laid-back family feel there, and the uniqueness of the people inspired a sense of freedom and strength within me.

Eight thirty rolled around quickly so I gave Anthony a call at his work. He suggested I meet him there where he would show me around the TV station and we could talk about the reservation.

Directions in hand, I was unable to find any public transport and my budget didn't allow for a taxi, so I walked.

It was only four or five miles, not a big deal, and I'd get to see more of the town. I got to see quite a bit of the main road although and by the time I got to the station I was exhausted.

I met with Anthony, who after showing me the station explained he didn't have any money and his car was broken down, so he wouldn't be able to take me out to the reservation, but he had a friend who might be able to help.

He promised to stop in at the hostel after work tonight and take me to his friend.

I was a little disappointed but took it in my stride. I wandered back into town and spent most of the day walking around looking at the shops and getting a feel for the area.

There seemed to be a huge portion of Indians there, who gradually over the day I discovered to be Navajo.

The Hostel owner was horrified later that day when he discovered I had walked so many miles.

"Weren't you told not to do too much exercise when you first get here; you're seven and a bit thousand feet up and the elevation is hard on you if you're not used to it" he said "make sure you drink lots of water." assuring me I needed to take it easy.   I took his advice as I was exhausted, and fell asleep as soon as my head hit the pillow.

It was only an hour or so later when Anthony knocked on my door. Quickly gathering my things together, we walked through town to 'The Church'. Anthony explained that this old church had been converted into a large house and a number of his friends lived there; it was known as the 'party-house'.

The biggest dog I've ever seen greeted us at the door; a wolfhound I was told, followed by a short, skinny, longhaired guy with glasses. He was almost 'geek' looking.

"This is Kenny" Anthony said as he introduced me.

Kenny led us into his room where a couple of people had gathered on his bed, all smoking pot.

Kenny told me how he didn't have any wheels at the moment either, but if he found some he would take me out to the reservation.

Before he managed to finish what appeared to me to be a lame excuse, a tall girl with dazzling long-lashes and messy, ringlet hair tuned up at the door to his room. She was on crutches with her entire left leg in plaster.

"Hi, I'm Nancy." She said with a huge smile.

I introduced myself and she explained to a puzzled Anthony how she had broken her leg skiing a couple of weeks ago.

I learned that everyone in the room had at some point spent time out on the reservation and all of them knew Titus, who I had to see.

It all felt right but it wasn't working very well so far as getting there. I suggested they give me directions and I would hitchhike out by myself but they wouldn't have a piece of that. There was one more option, and that was Anthony's friend Mark. Mark wasn't working at the moment so maybe he could hitch out there with me. He knew the way and I wouldn't be by myself.

Anthony, Kenny and I made our way a couple of blocks north to a small, old villa style house.

Mark came to the door straight away. He was large, clean-shaven, yet continued to fit with the 'hippy" theme going on with the rest of these guys. There was something about him though that made me feel uncomfortable. I didn't like the way he looked at me and during the discussion, I jumped on the opportunity for him not to help me out when he hesitated for a moment. Nevertheless he agreed to show me out there in the morning. It would have to be early though as it could take a whole day.

We set out at six o'clock the following morning. I had my heavy pack and discovered we had to walk to the outskirts of town to begin hitchhiking. It seemed a long way with that pack on but it was only about five miles. It did get very hot very quickly though and by the time we reached a place we could stop, I was exhausted.

We remained in that spot by the side of the main road out of town for a couple of hours; something I had never experienced before in my many years hitchhiking. I was lucky if I spent ten minutes in one place before I was picked up.

I was beginning to regret having Mark along.

Eventually some Navajos stopped in a truck, telling us to climb in the back.

At this point, the road only went one way so there was no point in asking us where we were going. As we drove towards the reservation the scenery changed dramatically. We quickly left the greenery of massive pines, and rocks for flat desert with the odd rolling mound protruding out as if it was about to burst into life.   There were areas of momentous reddish rocks jutting out of the ground, which Mark informed me, were called mesas and the Hopi villages were on the top of these mesas.

I sat back and took it all in. The new smells brought a sense of excitement and discovery with them and the apparent 'deadness' of this land we were driving through enlivened distant memories within me I was unable to consciously grab. I wondered how anyone could live out here. Not only did it seem that nothing grew on this land, but the heat would be difficult to handle.

Flagstaff had been a nice temperature as it was at such a high altitude.

We were dropped off in a small village where we again waited a couple of hours and continued to repeat this scenario a few more times.

Traffic was scarce on some parts of the road and we could go for almost an hour without seeing a single vehicle.

As the sun began to go down the temperature dropped exceedingly with it. Mark was convinced we would have to spend the night sleeping in the desert. I really wanted to get to Titus' so I sat quietly, asking my guides and helpers to take care of it.

Within ten minutes a truck pulled over and the kind gentleman agreed to drop us off at Titus' gate.

The beauty I experienced on that particular leg of the journey was beyond words. The sunset seemed to be different in the desert ~ more intense and vibrant, or maybe it was because I felt completely in-line with my purpose. I could feel the incredible forces with me guiding and protecting my journey. The overwhelming sense of purpose left me with a trust that fulfilled every part of me. All was divinely perfect.

Climbing out of the truck I wasn't able to see anything.

By this time it was pitch black and there were no lights to guide our way, just a gate entrance with a sign painted 'Titus" Farm' with a faded rainbow over the top of it.

Mark told me that the driveway was almost a mile long so after thanking our ride we headed up the dusty and extremely pitted driveway.

As we got nearer we heard the sound of barking dogs moving towards us and eventually they greeted us with much excitement. Mongrels without a doubt and they were soon followed by a tail-less cat that seemed equally excited at our presence.

A small, dim light appeared ahead of us and as we approached it I saw the silhouette of a thin, shirtless man standing with a plate in his hand, eating. The candlelight revealed the man to be standing next to a small wooden shack under a cover of tarps and propped up branches. Old ripped and tattered armchairs and couches sat outside, hinting at the potential for a large number of people.

The man put his plate down and looking at me with inquisitive yet hesitant eyes, introduced himself as Carlo. I noticed a sense of discomfort as he greeted Mark, asking him for his reason for this visit. Mark explained he was showing me the way and I proceeded to tell Carlo of my desire to visit. An invitation was extended for us to eat with him.

Carlo then took me inside to meet Titus.

Inside was as rough as the outside with just two very small rooms separated by a flimsy curtain.

The first room held a gas stove, large bench top, and storage shelves for many interesting and strange-looking food items, a coal-burning heat stove and Titus.

Titus' bed was a wooden slat that was no more than a long seat bench covered with a worn bear-hide.

Titus was lying down singing. It was a beautiful yet haunting sound. Carlo explained that Titus would drift in and out of consciousness but was jovial and happy and that he would often chant and sing in his native tongue.

Titus caught sight of me and sat up. He reached out his soft, wrinkled hand that had tilled hundreds of acres of fields, and with a big toothless said "Oh you are here, I've been waiting for you."

I caught what I thought was a twinkle in his eye before he lay down and began a new song.

Carlo handed me a plate of food and we moved back outside to sit and eat.

I was shown a small alter area next to all the seating where I could leave an offering if I chose to. This area was a circle of stones, filled with many beautiful items gifted from the numerous people who would pass through.

I took a small amount of each food item from my plate, and thanking the Creator for the abundance I receive, then placed it on the alter.

The food was Macrobiotic. Carlo explained to me how he had also been drawn to Titus through a dream or vision.

Originally from Indonesia, he had studied Macrobiotics and had run a Macrobiotic centre in Los Angeles. Grain was the basis of the diet with brown rice being the staple and beans being the main source of proteins.

Carlo had arrived on the reservation right after Titus had been knocked down and killed by his own brother. This brother had fallen into the darker ways and was attempting to take Titus' power. If he succeeded it would give him an increased lifespan.

Titus was resuscitated and Carlo nursed him back to health using the macrobiotic ways.

Carlo beamed with passion as he talked of macrobiotics and seemed even more excited when I asked for more information about it. Macrobiotics seemed to work for him. He was trim with well-toned muscles ~ good for someone his age which had to be mid-late thirties.

I noticed throughout the evening that Carlo appeared to avoid any contact with Mark and even encouraged him to head back to Flagstaff early the following morning.

I washed my plate in two large bowls of very cold water. One was for the first wash and the second was more of a rinse, then Carlo pointed out a place behind the shack to put my tent up, suggesting that it was the most sheltered place from wind and sun.

The toilet was a long-drop well away from the shack and I would have to use one of the flashlights kept on the outside bench to find it.

I was exhausted yet very excited. I felt strangely at home in this very foreign place.

As I was climbing into my sleeping bag, the zip on my tent was being pulled down and Mark popped his head through.

"What are you doing?" I said with a tone to let him know I was annoyed with his apparent disrespectfulness. I couldn't believe how rude he was.

"It's time to do the 'Wild Thing,'" he claimed with the sleaziest expression on his face that I have ever seen.

After refusing his offer he tried to explain that it would be payment for bringing me out here and that all the girls he helps out does it.

"You need to get out right now," I commanded.

He continued with his 'charm' until I became rude enough to ensure his retreat.

Finally, I was alone at last. I laid on the hard ground listening to all the noises of the desert. It was very quiet.

As I slipped in to a meditation I began to hear drum beats. I assumed it must be Carlo so I sat and listened to its magical sound. It began to pull me in to it. In no time at all I went deep into the earth.

The drumming gradually faded away and I heard the sound of wings flapping above me. They sounded huge, slow and gentle. I listened carefully trying to work out what it could possibly be. It circled over my tent then over the shack, then back over my tent again then off. I tried to get up to have a look but something kept me pinned in my bed and I knew I wasn't meant to see it. It sounded and felt like the wings had to be at least ten feet across or more.

As the sound of the wings faded off into the distance I began to see visions of Native American Life. It was as if a movie was playing the entire history of the Native Americans, and I drifted off to sleep with it still playing.

The calls of chanting woke me the following morning. Carlo was singing and I could hear a rattle as well. I quickly got dressed and followed his voice to find him at the front of the shack facing east. I stood, taking in the surroundings. It all seemed so different to last night. I could now see the drive I had walked up, winding its way through acres of cornfields.

Carlo then began to run, following the edge of the fields, with the dogs in tow.

Looking around, I saw we were indeed in the middle of the desert. Behind and off in the distance was a huge mesa. In-between was filled with small shrub plants and big washes where water once flowed.

I walked over to the small building and stepping under the tarp-covered shelter I noticed that the dishwashing water bowls on the bench I had used the night before were a murky grey colour and contained a plethora of strange looking insects.

I suddenly felt a little nauseous.

The sun had just come up so the air was still crisp. I looked around for Mark but I couldn't see his tent anywhere. I sat on one of the large armchairs and greeted the well-lived cat while Carlo continued his circuit around the crops.

As I sat there I wondered what I was to do now that I was here. I really hadn't thought too much about that. My main drive was to get here and I noticed some insecurities creep in which I quickly dispelled, reminding myself to trust it all.

Carlo walked towards me, asking how I had slept. I told him very well and that I had enjoyed his drumming. He told me he hadn't been drumming and hadn't heard any himself. I then told him about the wings and asked what it could have been. He seemed a little taken back. Owls were large but it was unlikely they would be there and even if they were they are silent flyers. He was fascinated but mystified.

Carlo asked me if I had had any problems from Mark and I filled him in on the events of the night.

"That's happened before with him. I don't like that guy, he's not genuine."

Carlo hadn't seen Mark at all that morning and he had been up before the sun.

Some blue corn batter mixed with leftover rice and beans from dinner last night was cooked up for breakfast and Carlo helped Titus walk outside where we ate.

As we were finishing up, a large brown truck pulled up. A little round face with glasses and a huge smile peered out at us from the same level as the steering wheel. The door opened and a tiny little lady climbed down from the monster of a vehicle.

Carlo introduced me to her. Rosa was Titus' daughter and was delivering a couple of things to Carlo.

Rosa lived in Hoteville, which was the nearest Hopi village to where we were. It was where we had to go to get water. They had a spring there that we would have to take empty bottles to get filled.

Carlo explained to me that we had about a gallon of water each for washing and drinking each week ~ hence the grey dishwashing water. Conservation was very important as we didn't have any way of getting to the spring until someone stopped in with a vehicle that wouldn't mind making the trip with us.

Rosa was gorgeous. She laughed a lot in true Hopi style and had a bright and open energy about her. She seemed very understanding of my pull to the area and invited me to the ceremonies in the plaza that weekend.

I was excited. I had no idea what they were but I knew they were special. Rosa said she would be back the following morning to pick me up.

Carlo made us all some Hopi tea that was made from the twigs off one of the shrubs out on the land behind us. It was hard to drink at first due to its very strong flavour, and both Carlo and Rosa had a good laugh from my expression at my first sip. After a cup or two it became quite pleasant.

I spent the rest of the day relaxing and becoming more familiar with my surroundings. Carlo filled me in with a few things I should know about the area and a general run-down on what was going on out there.

There were all sorts of friction and fighting between the people. Divisions had been created and now two main groups existed; the 'Traditionals', who were trying to live the old ways as given by the Creator and of which group Titus came under, and then there were the 'Progressives' who wanted to bring in western ways like power, water etc.

It was a big enough division to cause great animosity and even to the point of many of the Traditionals lives being threatened.

Witchcraft, Carlo went on to say, had become increasingly common on not only the Hopi reservation, but the Navajo's too.

Slowly as the people lost faith in their traditional ways, they began to use the dark forces more and more. Although the benefits are never lasting, they manifest instantly.

Unfortunately that leads to more and more abuse.

Titus then explained to me in broken English how his Creator had given him everything he needed, and the basis for their belief was trust. Trust that if they followed their traditional beliefs, they would be provided for. He then told me to pay attention as I moved around the reservation, to notice the crops. The suffering crops belonged to those suffering and struggling to keep the faith and trust. Many had stopped farming altogether and the number of true 'traditionals' could probably be counted on my fingers.

Titus then warned me about going to certain areas within the reservation, saying that as I was staying with him I would definitely be a target.

For some reason I wasn't intimidated at all by this new information. I felt very safe and protected on my path, and I was much too excited about the ceremonies the following day to let anything get in the way of that.

I had an early night, as I was quite exhausted.

Despite not doing much that day I think it was all starting to catch up with me.

I went back to my tent and noticed the staff I had made while in Mangawhai had lost all the white feathers I had tied to it. It didn't look like an animal had got to it as the binding was untouched. It was just that the feathers had all disappeared.

I was woken again the following morning at sunrise with the sound of Carlo's chanting and praying before he made his way around the crops.

It was another beautiful clear day, still a little crisp but it would be hot. I stepped outside my tent and noticed a large hawk feather on the ground at my feet. It felt like a gift. I knew this was to be placed on my staff.

I got my things together for the day and had just sat down to eat when I saw Rosa's truck pull in through the gate from the main road. A cloud of dust followed her up the long driveway and when she reached the halfway point the dogs caught on and raced to meet her with their most intimidating bark they could muster.

"Are you ready to see the 'Longhairs' today?" Rosa asked as she climbed out of her oversized truck.

"Oh, absolutely" I replied, not really knowing what the 'Longhairs' were.

I quickly finished off my oatmeal and Hopi tea while Rosa checked in on Titus. It was a five-minute drive to Hoteville from the farm and when we arrived in the village I was totally absorbed with this foreign and mystical world I had just walked in to.

Mud brick or adobe homes formed a close living environment. They were small but seemingly sturdy as I saw many people climbing up ladders to stand on their flat roofs.

There were small half-dressed children running around with dusty faces and matted hair. Small mongrel dogs and cats wandered around scavenging and attempting to play with the un-amused children. The most bizarre thing however was amongst all this apparent poverty and simplicity, was parked $30-$40,000 trucks and huge satellite dishes. It seemed completely out of place.

We pulled up and parked in front of one of these adobe homes. I was introduced to Martin and his wife and children as we all made our way to the plaza. I was told not to talk about the ceremonies during them. Any questions had to wait and be asked at a later time. Rosa then told me that she was sure I knew already but I should absolutely not clap at the end of a dance. Many visitors do and it is considered very rude, as the dances are not for entertainment. I assured Rosa I would be on my best behaviour.

We had just settled into our plastic chairs when the sound of bells and drums echoed through the plaza.

The adobe houses were built right next to each other as if it was one long building, and in the centre of the village they formed the outside of a large square. This square was called the plaza and all ceremonies took place there.

There were small gaps at the corners to move in and out of and people were piled right around the edges and on the rooftops. The women wore beautiful shawls and many of the men had their hair tied in a traditional manner with white cotton.

Drums, bells and rattle sounds soon filled the plaza. People were moving to the seats they had brought along with them and I could sense the excitement building.

Before long a breathtaking group of people came dancing into the plaza. Their regalia exploded with colour, feathers, bells, and masks beautifully painted. They had long black hair, half covering their faces, and coyote tails hung from their belts behind them.

Their whole body had been painted so not to look human at all. Bells were strapped to legs and they carried spectacular gourd rattles, both items providing extraordinary dimension to the entire sound as they pounded the firm dirt with every drumbeat.

The dance was slow and graceful yet powerful enough to believe the concept that they really were from the stars.

The chanting made my hair stand on end as it drove it's way to the very core of my being. These were the 'Longhairs' Rosa had mentioned.

I sat captivated for the rest of the day. The 106-degree heat didn't bother me at all. I was mesmerised by the beating of the drum that seemed to connect me to the earth. It felt as though it had become the heartbeat of the Earth.

The ceremonies continued until sundown with only a couple of short breaks. There were other Katchina dancers, as well as clowns; whose job it was to make fun of and humiliate whoever they could.

The entire day was enthralling and when I found out it would be happening again the following day I knew I would have to be there.

Rosa dropped me off at Titus' and agreed to pick me up in the morning for the second day of ceremonies. I stumbled off to bed exhausted, for a well-earned sleep.

I awoke the next morning to another hawk feather placed at my tent door. I knew this was a blessing or honour in some way but didn't totally understand it. I thought I would attach both feathers to my staff the next chance I got.

The second day was just as long and exciting as the previous one. Something about it all felt very comfortable to me.

I came away from the weekend raw from sunburn, and dehydration. Stupidity really but there was an inability to break away long enough to get some water.

I did however gain a new 'amazed and stunned' expression that was kept in place by the burnt skin.

Again I woke to find the third hawk feather at my door. When there was none the following day I knew it was time to wrap them on my staff. I felt a sense of protection from them as if they were a symbol to let me know I am not alone; a reminder somehow of my purpose.

It now felt right that the white feathers from New Zealand had gone and had been replaced with the 'messenger's'.

A week after the ceremonies I could still feel the drum beating in my heart. I was experiencing a calling that rippled through me with every step and breath I took. I wasn't sure what I was being called to do but I knew I was in the right place.

Days passed by effortlessly as I helped out on the fifty acres of corm fields.

We began the day at sunrise by going straight out into the fields. Titus and Carlo had shown me how to use their traditional planting stick and told me of the importance of praying for, and talking to the plants while working with them.

Most of the work at this time was weeding out tumbleweed. It was important to tell them that we weren't just being malicious by digging them up, but that they didn't belong there and needed to go.

'They must be blessed" Titus said.

At around nine o'clock we had breakfast, which normally consisted of oatmeal or leftover rice and corn mush from the previous night. Then it was back out into the fields until lunch.

Being the hottest part of the day, we would then wait until nearly four o'clock before finishing off the weeding. It wasn't an every-day job but did consume a good portion of the week.

The crops were vital to Titus and Carlo as it was all they had.

Corn was used as a gift for any occasion for the Hopi people and you were considered wealthy if you had your own supplies. Titus had at least three years supply buried in a pit on his land. Corn was definitely considered sacred by these people and the corn they grew was of an ancient variety. I was amazed at the huge variety.

Once the corn was picked and dried, some would be shucked and placed in bags for storage while others stripped and left on the cob for future use. It was always ground to flour, as you needed it, with simple hand grinders.

I enjoyed the time I spent working in the cornfields. It gave me time to notice things around me. It had been such an overwhelming sense of 'deadness' as I was on my way into the desert, but as I lived on and in it, it came to life.

I had stumbled across my first snake one morning on the way out to the fields and the pure beauty of it struck me. I'm not sure what type of snake it was but the colours were vivid and enticing. So much so that I reached down to pick it up. My mind kicked in and I decided that might not be the wisest thing to do so I sat and watched it for a few minutes before heading off.

I was amazed at the amount of life I saw around.

At the end of the day I told Titus of my encounter with the snake whereby he told me that it was quite an honour for me to see this particular type and it was a message to me that I was welcomed onto the land.

Being a Snake Priest, Titus informed me that the much more common rattlesnake, was very territorial and therefore they respected your living space. You were considered justified; within the Hopi's beliefs, to kill a snake that intruded into your home because of this rule. It all tied into the witchcraft practice whereby 'shape shifters' were able to transform themselves into animals of their choosing and more often than not, seek out a life to take.

Titus continued by telling me that the Creator had put a cure in every place he had put a venomous or dangerous creature.

In the case of the rattlesnake, throughout the Southwest the cure was the 'stinkbug'. He assured me that by eating this bug; which could be found under a rock, would save my life. I had to believe him as he had been bitten many times throughout his life during the sacred snake dance.

His eyes lit up and the tiny, frail body suddenly became vibrant and excited as he recalled catching, calming and dancing with the amazing creatures he affectionately called his brothers. He finished his story with a chuckle that quickly turned into song and trailed off as he drifted into another realm; one that was becoming more and more a part of his life every day.

I had the magnificent privilege of spending an afternoon with a group of Hopi lady elders shucking corn. This was special in that it was by invite only that you got to join them during this event.

Rosa had organised it for me and despite not understanding a word they were saying the entire time, I loved it. The process of shucking was not easy either, and I soon realised why these respected ladies had a nice coating of callus on their palms.

Later that day we sat and 'popped' corn. It didn't pop to the extent that we are used to but the result was deliciously crunchy, almost roasted nut-like. Rosa explained to me that this process would only work with specific sand from a particular area in the desert mixed with the corn as it heated over a flame.

Carlo and I wandered out onto the land surrounding the farm every evening to gather fresh greens and tea. I was shown which plants to pick and when, as they could be very bitter and inedible otherwise. I was constantly amazed at the amount of food available.

From the 'shack' we headed towards the huge mesa towering hundreds of feet straight up. What looked like flat, barren, dead, desert sand in between was speckled with sparsely placed branchy shrubs. These branchy shrubs however supplied us with a constant supply of leafy greens and Hopi tea that required a short period of palette adjustment.

I found I thrived in this environment despite having come from a small island surrounded with water.

I was now dreaming of water every night, in every conceivable way but there was something very special about the desert and I loved the simplicity of the lifestyle.

I spent some time with Titus' granddaughter.

Vana had just turned thirteen but had the soul of a very Wise One. She was able to see in to people's bodies, into the organs and bones and knew if they weren't well.

She was unsure about seeing things like this as well as her now frequent occurrence of visions, so I spent hours talking to her, working through her fears and uncertainties.

I felt an amazing presence within her and knew she would fulfil an important purpose in the future.

I met up with the local Medicine Man Burton. He towered above me but had the presence of a doe. We each discussed our own healing methods, with him explaining how he saw colour over parts of the body which then would be interpreted and treated with traditional medicine.

Burton was fascinated with my healing method and asked if I would accompany him on his next treatment, which happened to be in half an hour. I felt humbled in his presence, so to be asked this was truly an honour.

The journey was hot and rough.

We bumped and jerked down several dirt roads full of holes that resembled small craters.

Finally we reached the home of an old man and after a brief introduction, in the native language, Burton and I worked together for his friend. I tuned in and used the Divine healing energies to do what they had to and Burton used his skills and gifts to diagnose and treat.

This was the first time I had ever worked together on a healing and it was incredibly uplifting. I felt the strength and power moving around us. I sensed the presence of some Beings I knew to be Katchinas, as they surrounded us in a dance not unlike what I had experienced at the ceremonies.

I watched Burton as he worked, noting the colours around his friend then watching him follow up with chants, smoke and herbs. Burton placed the root of some plant in his friend's mouth, indicating to him not to chew. A small pouch was then given and placed around the old man's neck.

Burton reached down to pick up a large sack of corn that had been placed at the front door and it was put carefully into the back of his truck. I assumed this was his payment for treatment.   The old man acknowledged and thanked me before we headed back out the pitted roads to Hoteville.

I couldn't help but go over the entire healing in my mind, marvelling at the simplicity and flow of it. I felt that because this was so much a part of their culture, it was nothing spectacular or strange, and the effects would be noticeable. It was just assumed, I guess, that the healing had taken place. In a way it was the same in my culture where the majority of people place so much faith in doctors and just assume the medication will work.

I definitely felt as though I had stepped into another world. Every part of my reality had changed dramatically.

Upon arriving back at the farm I was told there would be a meeting of elders there that evening.

I helped Carlo clean and set up a meeting area for the ten people expected and within an hour the first elder arrived followed closely by the rest.

I made sure they were comfortable and had a cup of tea before making my way outside.

Over the last couple of weeks Carlo and I had made a huge pit where we had begun to make a permanent tipi. Around twenty feet high, it was half finished and roughly covered with tarps.

I gathered up some wood and placing it in the centre, lit a fire. The two resident dogs came and sat next to me followed by a couple brought by the elders.

Once a strong flame was established I sat back and felt inspired to meditate to bring forth energies to assist the elders in their discussions.

There had been so much turmoil within the community of late, the elders were doing their best to sort out ways of dealing with it.

Almost instantly I was aware of a beautiful man standing before me. Wrapped in a heavy woven cloak he introduced himself as Great White Raven Blanket. He told me there was something he would like me to pass on to the elders inside. I told him I would be honoured to but I wasn't going to interrupt the meeting. I would be willing to pass it on as soon as they finished.

Great White Raven Blanket proceeded to tell me of a time coming whereby all of the traditional ways would disappear. The future he said, would be in the children. They would bring through a new way of being but one that brought in the purity of the traditions as well. The ancient ways would be remembered once again by these children and it was important for the elders to not fight the change about them now.

I wrote the message out and handed it along with a drawing of its messenger to Carlo at the meeting's completion. Carlo handed it to Rosa who read it to the group of eager listeners.

I watched as heads nodded in acknowledgement of the truth given and appreciative smiles suggested they honoured my purpose.

Once the last of them had headed down the driveway Titus asked me to sit with him. He talked to me about the struggles they had been having not only in Hoteville but also in all of Hopi Land. He explained how each clan was responsible for their unique piece of information, handed down through the generations. It was well understood that being given a vast amount of information leaves room for variations through time ~ the 'pass it on' theory.

The Creator, in all his wisdom had dispersed pieces of knowledge and made the individual clans responsible to carry their one piece forward through time, unchanged.

Because of this type of community structure, it was forbidden to reveal information relating to your clan to any others, and the same with the individual villages. So in essence, gossip was forbidden.

Titus and the other elders were however very aware of what was going on with their 'people'.

As we sat bathed in the soft glow of the small coal-burning stove, Titus held my shoulders with his hundred and six year old hands.

With a grip that could pass for thirty year olds, he said, "You know you are as much Hopi as I am because Hopi is not about a breed of people, it is about what's in the heart. And you are Hopi at heart. Hopi means peace, but a peace that comes from the Creator. Many of those people out there who call themselves Hopi because they were born here, don't deserve it."

We heard a chanting outside that sounded similar to the Katchina's. Whoever it was, was dancing past the door to the shack, although it was so dark we didn't see anything ~ we didn't need to see anything, we knew it was a Katchina.

Titus laughed saying "They're here!, They've come to take me home!" With a hearty laugh he then began an uplifting yet haunting chant with gestures as if the Creator was directly before him.

Carlo brought out the peace pipe and introduced me to yet another sacred ceremony. It was a special moment and it felt as though we were being honoured.

7 SEDONA

Two months had passed and I only had another month before I was due in England to visit my Mother.

I decided to visit Sedona for a while before heading back to Los Angeles.

I said my goodbyes, packed up my backpack and headed down the long drive to hitchhike into Flagstaff and then Sedona. The sun was still making its way up; casting the most dramatic display of orange, yellows and reds I had ever seen. I knew I had to leave this early to ensure a ride.

Carlo had needed me to go to Flagstaff a few times during my stay to pick up supplies so I had learnt pretty quickly that there wasn't much traffic travelling up and down this road therefore I had to get out really early to catch the few travelling in to work.

Most of these were Navajo Indians whose reservation totally surrounded the Hopis.

On top of the mesa directly behind Titus' was all Navajo land.

My trips to Flagstaff were normally for the full day. If I was lucky I would get dropped of in the city and would go directly to Macey's for one of the coffees I found I was gaining quite a taste for.

Sometimes the trip would require three or four rides but for the most part I could reach Flagstaff by ten o'clock in the morning.

I had to make sure I was on the road by four to ensure getting back before sundown so I only had enough time for coffee, shopping for vegetables and a quick call to see how Anthony was doing.

Back on the road I was unable to put my pack down. I normally had to pick up carrots or potatoes so it was extremely, so much so that if I took it off I would never get it back on. This was a concern a few times when I was dropped off on the side of the road in the middle of nowhere with absolutely no traffic.

On one occasion I got to the point I thought I was going to die. I had run out of water very quickly, I couldn't take the pack off so I couldn't sit down or get any type of shade. It was looking very bleak. At a point of desperation I prayed; asking that someone come along and take me right to Titus' door.

Within minutes a Navajo lady pulled over and picked me up. After discovering where I was going she claimed she knew Titus well and would love to take me directly there.

I was really able to trust through situations like these.

Another time on the way back a man picked me up and was able to take me at least sixty-five of the ninety miles there. It all went well until a point I began to feel very threatened.

Something within me knew I was suddenly in a whole lot of danger. I asked the Creator for guidance and almost instantly understood I needed to change the focus of the conversation. Up until that point he had been asking a lot of questions about me.

Within a couple of minutes of asking him questions about his life I felt the energy shift back and I felt completely safe.

I had begun to trust another sense as well. In certain situations, normally while out in the desert by myself, a strange sensation would move through me. It was like a taste and a smell, combined with a gut feeling.

I knew without a doubt it was a warning, and I had sense enough to leave wherever I was.

Standing next to the road waiting for a ride gave me a moment to reflect on my time there.

I was truly blessed to have been led to such incredibly inspiring people. They showed me a new way of existing. I had become so aware of things around me and was inspired by my newfound connection with nature. I had met some fascinating people.

The 'troll' was the nickname Vana had given to Little Dan who was one of the Hopi elders. A beautiful man, Little Dan was well into his hundreds as well.

I met many wonderful Navajos despite being told before arriving at the reservation that I needed to steer clear of them as they're bound to "hit you on the head and rob you". Contrary to this I was asked to stay with many Navajo families.

They thought of it as an honour to have me in their home and share their way of life with me. I would have taken that opportunity as well, had I not been a vegetarian.

They, unlike the Hopi, were large meat eaters and part of the honour was that I would get to choose and then participate in the killing of the sheep to eat. I just couldn't bring myself to do it.

I noticed a car coming so I stuck out my thumb hoping they would stop. To my surprise I recognised the girl in the passenger seat to be Nancy whom I met when I first arrived in Flagstaff.

She introduced me to the girl driving the old white Chevy convertible as Dawn. They were the perfect image of freedom with their hair blowing in the wind.

"Where are you going?" She asked.

"I'm going to head to Sedona for a month or so." I told her.

"Well if you want to wait for ten minutes or so we just have to drop something off to Titus then we'll be heading back and can give you a ride."

I told her that would be fantastic. I threw my bag in the back and climbed onto the comfortably padded, old red leather seat. As we pulled up outside Titus', Nancy jumped out to greet Carlo and I noticed she no longer had the cast on her leg.

Twenty minutes, another round of goodbyes and we were on our way.

It was normally about an hour and a half trip back in to Flagstaff so we got a good chance to talk. The discussion turned spiritual quickly with Nancy mentioning seeing different things she wasn't sure about.

I told them about what had brought me out there and the healing I had done. I mentioned that I felt drawn to go to Sedona for some reason, which excited Nancy as she had felt a need to spend some time there as well.

It seemed that time stood still for us to become acquainted. Dawn had driven down from Santa Fe for a visit but wasn't as interested in the spiritual discussion as Nancy.

I booked into the De Beau Hostel for the night so I could get an early start for Sedona in the morning. I had promised to let Nancy know where I was so we could meet up before I took off.

It was about midnight before I got to sleep that night, as while I went out to get some dinner I bumped into a fellow 'Kiwi'. He was over for a short visit and wanted to go to Sedona the following day as well, so we decided to head there together.

He had never hitchhiked before and thought it would be fun.

Fun turned tortuous pretty quickly the next morning, as the first hill we had to encounter before getting to a suitable place to hitchhike was too much for my new friend Karl. He had a hard time with his pack and his shoes, the heat, and anything else he could think of.

Needless to say it took a lot longer than it should have. I was very grateful to the Navajos who picked us up, until they handed us a can of beer through the truck cab window. It was well before lunch, and from the swerving that took place from then on down the switchbacks, I could tell it wasn't the first can they'd had.

Despite the incredibly bad driving, sitting on the back of a truck gave us a whole other perspective on our surroundings, probably because you seem to be so much more a part of it and it wasn't just visual. The smell of pine and juniper mixed with wet red rock and sand became part of the picture, adding another layer to the visual experience.

The road, which leads from Flagstaff to Sedona down the canyon, was incredibly spectacular. Unlike the desert's dryness, we followed a large creek surrounded by lush green foliage and sheer rock faces.

At a point about two thirds down that all changed. The landscape opened up whereby the creek disappeared for a while and all of a sudden we were looking at huge red rocks, jutting out of the land in shapes taking on the appearance of church cathedrals, coffee pots and numerous others. But more than that, there was a powerful presence that these incredible natural sculptures seemed to add to.

We were dropped off at a Mexican restaurant that lured us in with bright colours and amazing smells.

Luckily Karl knew more about Mexican food than I did. Being my first experience there was a good chance I would have wound up setting something on fire.

I wasn't sure why we were being looked at so strangely but every waitperson seemed to leer at us as they walked by.

It was an enjoyable meal however, and in perfect timing when we stepped outside, Tony was just pulling up.

"You didn't go in there like that did you?" He asked looking at our bare feet.

We had taken our shoes off because they had become too hot and impractical.

"Well yes, it was too hot" I told him.

He laughed, shaking his head.

"You were lucky they even let you in. I know you're from New Zealand but you can't go round with bare feet here."

Back at Tony's house he set us up with a couple of mattresses and we spent the rest of the day talking about the area.

Apparently it used to be burial grounds for some Indian tribe. He wasn't sure which ones but knew that it was sacred enough for them not to live here.

Now it was a centre for 'New Agers', believed to be full of powerful energy vortexes. People come from all over the world to have the 'Sedona Experience'. It's incredibly wealthy. The town is owned and run by a group of retired Hollywood's elite. They get to stipulate they way you do business and the way you live to a certain degree.

"Did you see the buildings as we drove through town?" We both nodded in acknowledgment. "They all look the same. Heck even McDonalds have to fit the colour scheme; which is terracotta with green trim to blend into the red backdrop."

I could sense a tinge of resentment going on with him as he was telling us this.

While discussing my plans with Tony, I found out that as long as I was outside of city limits, I could set up camp anywhere.

I decided that the following day after Karl had left, I would hike up through some of the land behind Tony's to where he suggested was a good place to pitch my tent. He wasn't sure however if it was far enough to be outside the city limits.

The rest of the day was uneventful with Karl needing lots of recovery time before heading off the following day.

I arose early the next morning and making my way up through the land behind Tony's house, found a perfect place to camp.

I gathered up a selection of rocks to use as a fire pit surround. Tony had given me an old oven mesh tray to put on top of my fire and I dug a hole large enough for a decent sized fire and stacked the rocks around the edge as high as I could.

I knew it would be disastrous should a fire start here. There seemed to be a narrow lush area surrounding the river with the rest of Sedona just as dry as the reservation, with more and larger shrubs.

After a full day setting up camp and getting supplies I settled in to sleep for my first night in Sedona but found it too difficult as I could hear bugs underneath my tent scurrying along.

I know they were probably small but they sounded massive as they scraped the canvas as they moved. I could never really trust that there wasn't a scorpion in the tent with me.

I found a second-hand store the next day and stocked up with a pot, utensils and a few other necessities.

When I returned to the tent I could tell it had been opened. Lying at the entrance was a note from the local police informing me that I was not, in actual fact, outside city limits and I would have to move immediately.

What a drag I thought, I had just got set up so well. Following the instructions left by the officers, I wound up a long way from town but found an area next to what looked like an old riverbed. It was quiet and had quite a lot of larger shrubs that would be good protection from the elements.

I hiked back to my tent, packed it all up and made my way to my new home.

I was quite exhausted by the time I had finished as it seemed hotter here in Sedona than what I had experienced on the reservation.

Perhaps with the bigger shrubs came bigger bugs but I definitely didn't get any sleep that night either. There was a moment when I felt like I might drift off to sleep when the most horrifying animal sound came towards me. I had no idea what it was but it was heading straight for me and sounded like a whole lot of them, whatever they were. I didn't want to see so I closed my eyes and prayed. Within a minute or so the noise had gone right passed me although I could still hear it off into the distance.

It then became an even longer night as I sat inside my tent aware of every sound.

The sun came up at last and I was able to see my surroundings more clearly.

I got dressed and headed into the township. Maybe if I get a coffee I'll meet someone who can fill me in on that noise.

I found a small bagel shop on the main street so made my way inside.

The walls were covered with caricatures of all sorts of people. A few south-western styled clothes and jewellery were on display.

A middle-aged man with dark curly hair and glasses was behind the counter sorting and placing out pastries.

I waited until it looked like he could stop for a moment before ordering a coffee and blueberry bagel.

"Toasted with cream cheese please." I said feeling almost like a local. I was enjoying some of the new foods I was being introduced to.

I took a seat by the window and watched people come and go for at least ten minutes before making my way back to the counter to enquire about my missing coffee.

"Oh, sorry. I just got caught up, we're short staffed right now."

Without thinking I suggested helping out. He looked at me as if I was a miracle sent from God himself.

"We can't really pay anything but you will normally walk away with a reasonable quantity from the tip jar?"

"Done" I said and agreed to start straight away.

He introduced himself as Dan and quickly gave me a rundown on prices, till and procedure, and was then out the door.

I finished stocking the cabinets with bagels and pastries while trying to serve the growing serge of people coming in for their daily wake-up cup.

A young blonde-haired man came in and appeared quite shocked to see me there. I caught on that this was a place where the same people hung out on a regular basis.

"Leave her alone Tony" another man called out as Tony was obviously flirting with me.

I looked over to the see the man who had made the comment to be the one creating all the caricatures.

They were friendly enough and we joked around for the four hours they remained there. They quizzed me about New Zealand as they hadn't encountered anyone from there before and gave me a vague run-down on the area and assured me that the noise I had heard the previous night had to be coyotes.

"They are known as incredible hunters" Tony explained, "They send one coyote down the end of a wash…"

"What's a wash?" I asked.

"It's where during spring, water floods down from the mountain and cause huge gouges in the land. Anyway, once this one coyote is in place, the others herd a rabbit or other prey into the wash and then by making all that noise, they force it right down to the waiting coyote."

It hadn't even crossed my mind that the noise had come from a coyote. I was surprised and excited at the possibility of seeing these beautiful animals.

Dan popped in around four thirty to help. He told me that they had entertainment on that night so it would be a late one. I offered to stay on as I had nothing better to do and it would give me a chance to meet some more people.

It was a very friendly warm feeling in there with most people knowing each other.

Tony reappeared again just as the musician was starting his show. I had seen some very strange looking people wandering the streets of Sedona but this entertainer had a real 'hippy' look going on. He must have been in his fifties with long grey hair and beard.

"Hi, I'm Bastian, for those who don't know and I'm going to be playing some of my own music, along with a friend, hopefully, if they show up."

The music was nice, very folksy with a nice mixture of guitar and wooden flute. I had an enjoyable night, and topped it off by walking away with eighty dollars in tips.

The music had played until eleven thirty, and then Bastian convinced me to hang around to talk with him. He became excited when I told him I was interested in spiritual things and he gave me some pointers on camping out as he had lived that way for the last seven years.

He moved around constantly as it was illegal to be camped in the same area for any length of time.

Feeling positive, I made my way back to my tent at about one thirty in the morning. I hadn't thought about bringing my torch with me so I struggled to find my tent. Luckily there was enough moonlight for me to make out recognisable points along the way.   The underbrush was thick in places and a couple of times I was as surprised as small furry, snorting creatures that I was unable to identify moved very fast around my feet.

Exhausted, I changed into my bedclothes and knew I would sleep well. It had been a good day. Up until then my money had pretty much run out, so again, I was being provided for.

I had a lot to be thankful for.

I went back to the bagel shop the next morning as arranged, and decided to call Nancy to let her know what I was up to. She sounded excited.

"I'm going to head down there today. There's something I want to talk to you about."

"Ok" I said. "You know where this place is don't you?"

"Yeh, I'll see you in a couple of hours."

She arrived at a busy time so I handed her a coffee and asked her to find a seat.

It was about twenty minutes before I could get a chance to talk to her.

"So what's up?" I asked her.

She looked at me and I could feel her searching for what to say.

"I think there's something we need to do down here together." Her huge blue eyes sparkled as she talked and the dazzling smile never left her face.

"I agree. I certainly feel there is some land work to do down here. I've never done any before but I know that's what we'll be doing" I told her.

She was nodding and laughing as she had felt the same. "I know where we need to go too. It's an area that's been used for a lot of cult ceremonies, you know, where real bad stuff has gone on."

It felt right, within me, so we agreed that she would come back tomorrow and at 11am we would head out to do some earth healing. I was excited to say the least. It all felt so right and easy.

The remainder of the day drifted by as if I was suspended within a cloud, just watching everything going by without being connected to it. Something had connected within me and I knew for sure I was where I needed to be.

Tony and Bastian stopped in to talk for awhile and then I made it back to my tent by about six pm.

I was almost too excited to sleep but before the anticipation had a chance to keep me awake, I was bombarded with energy. A high-pitch ringing came with the presence of some unpleasant entities.

Despite surrounding myself with light and calling in protection from the Brotherhood of Light, they continued to harass me for hours. I could feel them trying to probe my mind.

Finally after really becoming focused on clearing the energy, I fell asleep exhausted.

I woke up feeling quite shattered but managed to get myself together enough to make way to the bagel shop where Nancy and I had arranged to meet. It was a good thing too because if ever I needed a coffee it was now.

Nancy pulled up within a few minutes of me arriving so we sat down to discuss our plans. I filled Nancy in about my crazy night and surprisingly she said she had experienced the same, and had felt someone was trying to get information from her. Brushing it off, we headed out into the desert.

It was already starting to get hot so we took plenty of water with us.

We got as close to the site as possible in Nancy's four-wheel drive, but eventually had to abandon it and continue on foot.

Nancy said she had been there a few years before and was sure she would still remember the way.

Just as we had gathered our water and started moving away from the vehicle, we saw a deer watching us.

She stood for a moment as if making sure we saw her, then turned and walked slowly in the direction we had begun to move.

Feeling this to be a blessing, our confidence and purpose was strengthened.

Not more than two minutes later we were surrounded with the same energy as we had experienced the night before.

Despite our desire, we could feel our plans had been sabotaged and we would have to try again another day. We knew these energies were interfering with what we needed to do and despite not being able to see them, we felt their presence.

Accepting defeat this time, we vowed not to discuss the next one and simply allow our guidance to take us where we needed to be in the moment.

It was clear we were both a little disappointed at our first attempt so we stopped at Nancy's favourite Mexican restaurant for lunch on our way back, and decided to meet again the following day.

Beautiful clear skies greeted me the next morning. In fact I hadn't witnessed a drop of rain yet, which was good for me in the tent. It was a cheap thin tent and I wasn't sure it would hold up in any rain.

Nancy turned up on time again and I arranged with Dan to work the night shift as Bastian was playing again; this time with another well-known musician in the area that I had been told "You just have to see."

The roads were quiet as we headed out of town. I began to tune-in to get a feel for where we needed to be. As I began to feel pulled to a certain area I could see Nancy felt the same. We didn't talk about it; instead we just went there.

We wound up climbing a steep treacherous hill of the soft Sedona red rock. The road was horrendous with pits large enough to give the four-wheel drive a hard time.

Almost an hour passed before we felt we had arrived.

High above Sedona we looked down from finely perched red rocks to see a dome of energy smothering the whole town.

I noticed now how different I felt away from the township. My head was clearer. I realised the magnitude of the energy produced by the vortexes there and vowed to leave the town at least once a fortnight to clear my energy field.

In that moment I also understood why so many people living there had become rather 'crazy'. The energy was so intense it amplified absolutely everything, causing many to loose it. I understood also one of the sounds I had been hearing to be the sound of the vibration there.

What a truly incredible place. No wonder it needed some healing. Everyone has been going to it for such a long time to use its energy without replenishing or balancing it.

We climbed to the highest point of the rock that for me was an amazing achievement in itself, but height felt different as long as I was connected to the land.

Directly below us was a massive flat, round rock. It was large enough for a sizeable spaceship to use as a landing pad.

Sedona certainly had a name for being an area producing a high numbers of sightings.

Both of us were looking down at the platform when a deer appeared and began to make its way up the stepped sides and vulnerably stood right in the centre of the large platform. Tears came to our eyes in recognition of a guide on our journey.

I felt a beam of energy enter me from above and upon tuning in to it, I felt the presence of the Brotherhood.

I allowed the energy to flow through my body, then down deep into the earth; becoming an anchor for the energy. I felt the earth connecting with me, and energy flooding in to strengthen the area. My awareness connected that the energies in this area had been used inappropriately and needed to return to its pure form, which is what we were there for.

There was a struggle within me with this healing work. I felt such a desire to work and 'do' something, it was hard to stand back and allow it all to happen. I knew my only responsibility, as a Light-Worker was to be that of a channel and anchor, for that is the greatest thing, but in a sense I didn't feel as though I was doing enough. I wanted to get more involved.

The energy pouring through me had subsided and the Brotherhood let me know we had completed our task.

Climbing back into the vehicle, Nancy told me how she had seen a beam of gold light descending from the sky and going directly into the top of my head. It had freaked her out at first but then she realised what was happening.

She hadn't experienced anything, but was aware of the Katchinas around her.

I thanked all involved and we made our way back down the winding hill.

Halfway down the pitted road, just as Nancy had navigated around a difficult and dangerous corner, a huge black helicopter appeared out of nowhere to the left of us. It had come up over the ridge and was promptly followed by two more.

All three of them hovered next to us, with the first one swinging around to point huge machine guns directly at us.

They were so close I could see the face of the man closest to us. It was a clear view because the side door was open. I will never forget that face as it didn't look or feel to be of this world. It was human shaped alright but there was something different about it.

Calling upon my inner strength, I smiled and waved at him while sending an abundance of Love.

As quickly as they appeared, they flew off. We watched them go higher in the sky then disappear in a flash of light as if they had never existed.

Nancy pulled over and we discussed what we had just seen to gain some grasp on reality. We had both seen the same thing.

Instinctively we knew they had intended to stop the energy work we had done, but because we had gone on intuition, by the time they found out where we were, it was too late.

Now we felt like warriors! It was incredibly exhilarating to know we had been doing something so important to create such a reaction.

I talked to Nancy about faith and unconditional Love for the remainder of the trip down the mountain. I felt that we would be tested if we were to do any more of this work together and we needed to make sure we knew where we stood in ourselves so we would be strong enough to deal with it.

Just before we reached the bottom of the hill and while I was explaining the real essence of the word Love, Nancy shrieked, then suddenly pulled off to the side of the road.

"You've got green light coming out of your eyes!"

I calmed her down, letting her know that she was just seeing the essence of who I was. I told her not many people had been able to see those levels of me.

Once she felt comfortable with the fact that I wasn't going to turn into some freaky alien, she was able to continue driving.

The whole experience of the last couple of days had been out of this world so I understood her reaction.

The following few days passed by with nothing eventful happening.

Bastian was coming on stronger, wanting me to go swimming at the local waterhole with him and Tony's advances were so obvious it was hard to take him seriously. I knew it was probably a cover or front he put on because of insecurities but I wasn't interested in buying in to it. If he wanted to go out he would have to ask me straight out, not continue with the not so subtle suggestions that could be blown over easily.

Nancy and I got together a few more times, going to remote areas and doing the same thing; just being present to be an anchor for this new energy needing to be infused.

As always, the presence of a deer greeted us, and it was no exception on the eighth excursion.

Having thought we would be going somewhere close, we were a little unprepared for the distance we had to walk this time.

Sure enough the deer was there to greet us and we made our way through tough desert terrain.

Two hours later we came to an area that looked like a massive hole in the ground that could have been made by a meteor or even pass as a volcanic crater. I felt we had arrived at the correct spot so we found a comfortable spot to sit and wait for the next step.

I began to hear laughter. Not human laughter but etheric.

Nancy heard it too and before I could call upon the Brotherhood, the crater we were in was bombarded with dark blue beams of light that exploded the ground where they hit.

Directly above us was what looked like a web of contrails being woven by invisible craft.

Energy began to be pressed down on top of us as if it was trying to close us in, so I called out to the Brotherhood for help.

Instantly, four big clouds began moving in towards the centre of the crater underneath the contrails. They moved together and at the moment of converging in the centre to create a cap for this giant hole, there was a remarkable lightning storm.

Bright blue electrical energy darted out everywhere, charging us and I'm sure anything else anywhere near.

I sat in total awe of what was going on before me, thinking it was as if I was caught up in a science fiction movie. It was hard for me to believe, let alone anyone else.

I could tell that Nancy was experiencing a similar surreal perspective and despite feeling so much, we found it difficult to find words for what we were experiencing.

One of the elders then communicated to me that the mission was complete and as a bonus, we were going to be given a gift. The familiar supportive energy swept through me, guiding me to head in a particular direction.

Once over the ridge of the canyon, we saw the deer waiting for us and knew it would lead us out safely, as we were well and truly lost.

The sun was on its way down so it was getting considerably cooler.

Just as we were about to give up and assume we were imagining things with the deer, we came across the ruins of an Indian settlement. It was totally undisturbed.

It was definitely a wonderful gift to be lead there.

We sat and absorbed as much of it as we could before quickly making our way back to the vehicle before we lost all light.

Both of us were overwhelmed.

Once back in Sedona and consuming burritos at the now regular Mexican joint, we were able to talk about it.

We both felt as though there would only be one more healing to do and I was due to leave within a few of days, so it would have to be tomorrow.

I however wasn't concerned about leaving.

England certainly wasn't a place on the top of my list to go to and I had run out of money. At this point I wasn't even able to get to Los Angeles to catch the plane.

I headed back to my tent for a good sleep and to prepare for the next adventure.

As I was walking up the road, Barry pulled over offering me a lift. Barry had become a good friend but wanted a lot more.

Despite his lovely personality, heart and advances, I just wasn't interested. I wanted to maintain our friendship however, as we enjoyed each other's company. He was interested in spiritual things although had a bit of a hard time accepting some of the things Nancy and I had told him of our adventures.

I accepted his offer for a ride although he could only take me a short distance before I would have to walk.

I gave him a rundown on the day's events and he told me we were crazy.

"See you tomorrow. Are you working?" He asked.

"Yep. The late one. There's a new singer performing who I'm told is excellent."

"Ok, Bye." I said and disappeared into the desert.

Sunstroke had almost overcome me as I lay in my tent when a passing hiker called out to me.

"Hi, is anyone in the tent?"

I poked my head out to see a young athletic guy looking quite agitated and concerned.

"Do you know you are right next to this rattlesnake pit?" He was pointing to a big hole in the side of the wash just three feet away from the entrance to my tent.

"No, I didn't have a clue, Thanks."

With that he disappeared through the shrubs towards town.

I wasn't really concerned about the snakes; in fact I thought it was probably some way of Titus keeping an eye on me.

He had talked about the connections to the animals of the respective clans and I felt safe because of this connection with him to the snake clan. I sent out thanks to the snakes who hadn't disturbed me, and drifted into a deep and satisfying sleep.

We were beginning to feel anxious as we met for morning coffee. Nancy knew as well as I did that we were going to be lead to the most difficult site yet.

After an invigorating dose of caffeine and a couple of straight-out-of-the-oven pastries, we made our way in total uncertainty but complete knowing.

Driving through a dark narrow canyon was enthralling. We were in the middle of nowhere; further into the harsh environment than we had been before, and despite our trust and faith in what we were doing, we felt vulnerable.

We had to do some serious off-roading to get this far and hoped the way out would become more obvious to us than the way we had come so far.

There were no homes anywhere near and no need for anyone to be around, and yet in several places, frail, unkempt men were sitting along-side the small dirt tracks we were following.

They watched us with lifeless, sinister eyes, peering in to us as if trying to get a glance into our Soul. They knew who we were and why we were there. They were merely the gatekeepers, or lookouts and their presence only inspired us to put up more protection and connect in to our higher energies even more.

It was several hours before we finally reached our destination. Opening up before us was a large area with steadily inclining red rock mounds on either side. The flat open area was quite different to that around it as it was void of all life. Not one shrub was growing and what should have been the typical red-toned rock, took on a dull grey hue.

The area had a familiar stench of skin-crawling dark forces we had become accustomed to on these missions.

On the sides of what appeared to be the entrance to the clearing, were gigantic rock pillars. While they were naturally weathered, they took on the uncanny resemblance of aliens we had come to know as 'the Greys'.

Nancy laughed nervously while trying to cover the obvious hesitation of moving forward through these ominous 'gates'.

I sat down, and feeling a compelling desire to connect with the Brotherhood for guidance, I asked Nancy to join me in a couple of minutes meditation.

I was overwhelmed with images and vision. I felt myself moving into the Earth beneath us. I was travelling through tunnels filled with people scurrying around. I saw large rooms of mechanical equipment and many things not of this world.

It was then that I realised some of these people were not of this world either.

Further observation revealed others in military uniforms.

We were above an underground base. I had heard people talk about an underground military base here somewhere but had thought the idea absurd. It was talked about around Sedona alongside discussions about the cults and human sacrificial ceremonies.

I opened my eyes to see Nancy looking around. She hadn't seen anything, but when I described what I saw she agreed it was what she had felt as well.

A big decision had to be made at that point. If we were to go further in, we would wind up underground without a doubt. It felt ominous so I suggested to Nancy that she might want to let someone know where we are before we do this because after discussing it, we both felt there was a good chance we wouldn't return.

Reluctantly we headed back to Sedona.

Barry was sitting at a table by himself when we walked in to the bagel shop. I knew I could trust him and he had already been informed about what we were doing so I decided to tell him about our plans for the following morning.

"That's insane. Why are you doing it?" He said.

I filled him in. "We have to. It's our purpose. You've heard about all the stuff they do at those underground bases haven't you?"

"Well yeah." He replied hesitantly.

"Well if we don't go in there to try to help stop it, who do you think will? Besides, so far we've only had to be present and allow the energy to anchor, then the brotherhood take over and complete the work."

This eased his mind enough to agree that should we not return the following day by five pm, he would notify authorities.

The remainder of the day went by slowly. I enjoyed the night at the shop with some great entertainment.

Bastian and Tony were there and I noticed they had become quite hostile to each other over the last couple of weeks. Tony had become quite upset when he discovered I had gone out with Bastian one evening and Bastian didn't like me spending any time with Tony at all.

I tried my best to keep it all civil and make use of the dwindling time I had left.

The owners of the shop were appreciative of my help and asked me to return at any time.

"You have to come back for a 'white Christmas'. It is so beautiful here then. You can stay with us if you like and you've always got a job here."

I thanked them as we were locking up for the night and I assured them I would do my best to come back. I suggested I might not be leaving at all if I couldn't get to Los Angeles. I only had eight dollars left, which was certainly not enough for that trip.

I knew there was no point getting stressed about it. If I was meant to go, it would happen. I wanted to see my Mother but I no longer considered my life to be about me. I had made a commitment to my spiritual path, and because I couldn't always see the bigger picture, I had to trust the events and opportunities happening around me.

As I had done at the beginning of this journey, I put it to God or the Creator that it was out of my hands.

I had offered to help Dan out in the morning during the six am rush, which he gratefully accepted so I was up nice and early.

I stepped outside my tent to discover a series of large cat paw prints around my tent. I had no idea there were any mountain lions in the area. Even bears didn't come down this low in elevation.

I spent a few minutes looking around to see if I could see anything but I didn't feel threatened or unsafe in any way so I carried on.

Just as Nancy pulled up to the café door, an attractive middle-aged lady came up and asked me if my name was Leigh and if it was me that needed to get to L.A. When I told her it was yes, to both questions, she handed me a plane ticket.

I offered her a coffee while she continued to explain how she had bought the ticket for her daughter to visit her Father in California. Her daughter had decided not to go after all, despite her pleading.

"I can't use them and they are not refundable. So if you can't use them, they will go to waste."

I opened them up to see they were scheduled to arrive at the airport one hour before my flight was due to take off for England. I didn't need any more signs or proof to believe in a Divine presence than that.

Dan had overheard the conversation and commented how a new supply of bagels needed to be picked up from Phoenix the following morning and if I went down with his wife, I would get to the airport in plenty of time to catch the plane. I thanked them both and discovered Dan had called around all his friends the previous night, asking if any were making a trip west and had been responsible for contacting the lady now sitting in front of me.

I quickly called my Mother to let her know I would be arriving as scheduled before heading back out to the underground base with Nancy.

The second time in to the area was easier until we arrived at the entranceway. We looked around, making sure we were in fact at the right place because there was now a huge gate across the entrance.

A large roughly painted white sign hung precariously from the excessive amounts of barbed wire hanging from heavy wooden posts.

"You are HERE," it read, with a huge red 'x' marking this position on a simple hand-drawn map. It then commanded, "Turn around and go back NOW."

A couple of hundred metres beyond the entrance was the silhouette of several soldiers. Dressed in dark uniforms from head to foot, they threatened us with the presence of readied weapons.

Stunned, we sat on a nearby rock to plan our next move.

We could see a fence running the entire perimeter of the clearing. It had to be hundreds of acres miraculously fenced off over night.

Before we could make any decisions, one of the soldiers came up to the fence and demanded we leave immediately.

I recognised him to have similar features as the man in the helicopter on our first healing journey.

Fighting my natural desire to send a barrage of questions his way, I sensed his seriousness and moved back to the vehicle and got in. Nancy followed as he kept his gun pointed our way.

Once we had covered a few miles, Nancy pulled over to get a drink of water. I could see she was shaking so I turned of the ignition and moved around to her side of the vehicle.

It had been an intimidating experience and we hadn't been able to do what we felt we need to but I felt it was OK.

"What do you think we should do?" Nancy asked.

"I think we probably need to leave it. From the looks of it the fencing goes right around, and they were expecting us, so I doubt we'll be able to get in any other way without them seeing us. I'm not sure what it was about but it doesn't look like we're going to get in. Let's just sit and meditate for a little bit and see if we can do anything from here"

After ten minutes I could feel an intense energy had been anchored in the area and Nicki's shaking had started to subside and colour returned to her face. It felt good to move on.

Despite not being able to do what we thought we would, I felt it was OK.

We made our way back to town slowly, reflecting on our entire experience together.

We would miss each other.

The month had gone by extremely quickly but I had formed some wonderful friendships during that time.

"What am I going to do when you've gone" Nancy commented. "I won't be able to do this on my own, you're going to have to come back."

As Nancy was talking, she was forced to use the brakes to their full limit when a deer walked calmly onto the road in front of us. The very beautiful and somewhat unconcerned doe looked at us for one of those brief moments that seemed to linger for eons, before continuing across and through into the shrubbery on the other side of the road.

This was a sign that somehow, our work had been completed.

We laughed and sang together as we navigated the rough desert terrain back to civilisation. I soaked up as much of the surroundings as I could; implanting within my mind the varied colours of the dirt, recalling the delightful aromas of juniper mixed with dirt and tar after a monsoon shower, and the sounds of the incredible wildlife blessing my life experience to this point.

I had only just seen my first roadrunner the previous day and was surprised at how small they were.

The little creatures I had almost stepped on early in my stay in Sedona, I discovered to be Javalinas.

The mountain lions had made their presence known, and the coyotes used the wash right next to me every night to secure their feast. This was my kind of place.

There was a connection here for me.

The place and the people had become very close. I would miss it.

With my gear packed up I made my way to Dan and Debbie's house.

We would have to leave at 4am for the journey to Phoenix. Nancy was waiting for me when I arrived. She looked a little panicked.

"Fires have broken out, it's all over the news. Every place we did the healings in has broken out with fire. Fire fighters and helicopters are out there as we speak trying to put it out. What have we done?"

I took a deep breath then closed my eyes to call upon an Elder of the Brotherhood to explain. He came in quickly; assuring me it was Ok. It had to happen this way he said, and that it was the final part of the cleansing we had activated.

Regardless of his assurance, we both felt weird about it.

I asked Nancy to keep me informed as to how it ends up as I climbed in to Debbie's huge purple Oldsmobile.

It was a good two-hour trip with Debbie needing to be back by eight. Plans were tested however when a massive storm was moving in to hamper any thoughts of having a smooth trip.

Debbie assured me we would make it and sped up.

The storm hit us like a cyclone and I was horrified to find out the windshield wipers didn't work.

Debbie however continued her obsessive objective of reaching Phoenix within an hour and a half.

Being visually impaired at the best of times with glasses as thick as a chopping board, and having observed her inability to ensure giving the correct change to customers in the shop, I felt a little uneasy.

I closed my eyes for the majority of the trip and prayed it all be over quickly.

The storm remained severe for the duration of the trip so I was relieved when we pulled up to the airport in one piece.

Being late however, meant I needed to be on the other side of the airport within ten minutes. Luckily check-in was quick, so I bolted through the complicated building, navigating my way through a vast amount of people.

I had almost made it to my gate and approached the final security checks when two guards who had been sitting talking to each other start running after me shouting, "Stop right where you are!"

As they didn't acknowledge me when I arrived, I assumed they weren't working so I carried on through at great speed to catch the plane now boarding.

I turned around to see one of the guards chasing me with a gun drawn while the other one was on his radio calling in the event. I explained I didn't know I had to stop and I was about to miss my plane whereby the first officer had a quick look at the small handbag I was carrying and thankfully suggested I move on quickly.

I was seated next to a young dark-haired guy who reeked of alcohol, and had the overall appearance of a strung-out rock star,

I pretended to sleep.

My efforts only lasted until a cup of coffee was brought around at which time my new friend decided to engage me in full conversation. He decided that when we arrived at L.A., I should change my ticket for a later flight and go to a party with him.

His voice became a monotonous drone in the background as I recalled my time in this mighty country. How much it had changed me in such a short space of time, and how much else there was out in the world for me to experience.

These thoughts generated such an excitement within me I was hardly able to contain it. Luckily by the time we arrived in L.A. my neighbour had forgotten his original offer and I was able to move off effortlessly as he tried to convince the hostess to join him for dinner.

8 TO THE MOTHERLAND

My mother and I had always had a bumpy relationship, to put it mildly, but I was always glad to see her.

It had been around five years since her last trip to New Zealand and that visit ended in disaster when our personalities and expectations of each other clashed.

It was on that trip I confronted her with feelings I had carried with me from childhood.

"Why don't you love me? Why have you never loved me?" I asked her.

She looked genuinely shocked and hurt. "I do love you, so much. I have been realising a lot of things lately though and I realise I didn't know how to love. My Mother never showed me love so I didn't know how to express it."

I felt like a little child again as I realised my tears were a desperate attempt to receive her love.

"I always felt as though you resented me." I said.

"I guess I did in a way." She responded. "I didn't want children straight away but I had a lot of pressure from your Father's family, and mine, to have you all. I really wanted to carry on with the fashion design and then raise a family. I wanted you, and when you arrived you were the greatest gift, but I probably carried a lot of resentment towards the whole situation. But never towards you."

She went on to tell me that her stepfather had sexually abused her. I could tell it was difficult for her to tell me and even more so when she claimed her Mother had known about it but did nothing. Her Mother's justification for it was that at that time, she didn't want to risk loosing her husband. Having three children to support, she instead kept quiet and turned a blind eye.

I felt sad for my Mother to have had to deal with that and carry it through her whole life.

She had never been able to tell anyone as when she had tried as a teenager, she was told she was lying and to never talk about it again.

She had endured that abuse her entire childhood until she was old enough to leave home at sixteen. Hearing this gave me a sense of understanding.

My Mother had always felt distant to me and now I could see why. She had to retreat within herself to deal with the pain ~ something I understood all to well.

I began to feel closer to her immediately.

Standing at the arrival gates, she looked as beautiful as always. I was always impressed with the pride she took in her appearance. Her clothes were always smart with many being her own designs.

She had always filled our Christmas stockings with clothes she had made. Looking back, we probably didn't appreciate her as much as she deserved. She is a special lady but totally misunderstood.

"Hi. How was the flight?" She said as she gave me her usual hug from the side.

I could tell she was disappointed with what I was wearing.

Before I left Sedona, Debbie had given me a couple of the south-western style dresses she had for sale in the bagel shop.

I knew they would be comfortable for flying but it did make me look somewhat like a bag lady.

I let it blow over and told her she looked fantastic.

It was an hour and a half drive to where she lived with Peter.

They had met in New Zealand and moved to England when my Mother became interested in tracking some of her family roots.

She hadn't known a lot about her biological Father as he died during the war when she was only three years old.

Unfortunately, her Mother and stepfather weren't helpful with any information, so she felt she needed to find out for herself.

Peter looked great even though I knew he didn't enjoy England at all and was waiting for the first opportunity to head back to New Zealand.

He had spent a lot of time on yachts before leaving the country and as far as I knew he hadn't had the opportunity to sail since then.

They were living in a beautiful old brick Manor. It was probably common for the area, but to me, coming from such a young country, it felt ancient. It was bursting with memories and secrets. I couldn't wait to look around in the morning.

They filled me in on all the gossip and I got a clearer idea of their life. Peter worked for the owners around the property and my Mother worked in the local town doing office work.

I unpacked, placing my clothes into a dressing table squeezed into the corner of a tiny room.

Barely enough room for a single bed, it had served as badly needed storage space. I found my way up the narrow staircase to the living room. Small was an understatement for the entire living quarters. Peter told me that it was typical for workers quarters and they were lucky they were allowed to use the main entrance. He went on to explain it wasn't uncommon for workers to be restricted to the servant's entrances at the back of the main buildings.

The décor suited its setting, with very English florals and patterns. The musty smell was reflective of the hundreds of years worth of history held within these sturdy walls.

After dinner I sat with my Mother to fill her in on my exciting journey so far.

During this discussion she told me that she had cancer.

Silence filled every nook and cranny of the room as my mind analysed what I had heard.

"Well what type of cancer and how bad?" I asked, not even sure where to start.

"It's breast cancer but it's in the early stages so it looks promising. I'm following a system developed in Mexico that's had amazing results. I'm not worried about it and the doctors don't see any need to remove anything, I just wanted you to know." "Thanks. Is there anything I can do?" I asked.

"I would like it if you could do some healing that you do and heal me." I could tell she believed I could do that.

"Mum, I can't heal you. You have to do that. All I can do is be a channel for the healing energy. You have to be the one doing the work." I was having a horrible feeling she didn't want to be healed. She wanted me to fix it. I felt trapped in a horrible place where I wanted to help her but I wasn't able to. It was devastating to me and couldn't bring myself to say no.

"We'll work on some techniques while I'm here but I need you to put out to the Universe the desire to be healed and the belief that it is possible."

I had a hard time sleeping that night. My desire was to help my Mother, but my purpose and inner knowing wouldn't allow me to. I meditated, asking her guides for support so I could then help her.

She needed to be prepared to look at some issues in her life that had caused the cancer. I believed dis-ease was caused by emotions held on to, and buried.

I finally drifted off while still in a deep meditation; enclosed in a beautiful pearl-luminescent healing room, filled with Angels and guides, all assisting my Mother.

Over the next month we took some wonderful trips around England with my Mother taking me to most of the power places of spiritual interest.

Brief moments of fun were overshadowed with tension.

Many issues arose during my stay with her and it felt as if we constantly pushed each other's buttons.

My older brother Stuart was now living in Oxford running a pub and had asked if I would come up and help him out for a while.

It paid pretty well as all living expenses were taken care of.

I know my Mother wanted me to stay with her longer but I thought I could save enough money to get back to America and buy a van to get around and live in.

I had decided to try to make the journey back to Sedona by Christmas so I had about five months.

Oxford was a pretty town and I spent many hours sitting outside the old buildings in the bitter cold, drawing the fascinating stonework.

For the most part I enjoyed the pub work. It was what I was good at and in this case it was temporary, so tolerable.

The pub patrons gradually revealed an attitude that wasn't just personal to me, but applied to all New Zealanders and Australians.

In their drunken ramblings they cursed us claiming we were taking all their jobs. This only became a problem at closing time when they refused to leave unless asked by a 'true Pom'.

I also got to see how we were typically employed before them as we were hard workers.

I supplemented my bar wages doing tarot readings at the local market during the weekends.

It was an outside market and often my fingers became so frozen in the bitter sleet cold I could barely shuffle the cards. At this point I also made a decision to loose the extra weight I was carrying around.

Exercising was not enjoyable for me but I pursued it with a passion. Every morning I would ride Stuart's bicycle through Oxford, and then did a series of resistance exercises.

I was also rigidly keeping to the macrobiotic diet I had learned from Carlo. Within two months I had lost two stone and was feeling so good I went out and bought a pair of very tight new jeans.

I had always skimped on clothes. During my early teens my Mother had a design and sewing factory set up in our garage. She employed a couple of ladies and I was dragged in to help after school and during the weekends.

It was mainly monotonous straight sewing but I did get to see the value of clothing and exactly how cheaply they can be produced. Despite knowing and understanding the value of designers and retailers, I think that knowledge stuck with me.

I am much more content finding a good deal at the second-hand store, knowing also that the money is going to a good cause.

So it had to be a pretty big occasion for me to buy brand new clothes, and loosing that much weight was definitely one.

I'm not sure why I had always struggled with my weight.

I knew I was sensitive and I did sometimes eat to protect myself from energies I didn't understand; however I had learnt a lot about energies since my decision to quit the job at the club.

Meditations had taken me into realms where total understanding of energies existed, so that on my return to this reality I retained the knowledge but I was sometimes unable to express it to other people. At these times I knew I craved chocolate and more often than not, complied with those cravings.

Regular phone calls to the Hopi reservation kept me up to date with everything going on there and it was during one of these calls I learned of Titus' passing.

I sent out a prayer and immediately felt his presence with me. What a wonderful Soul he was and still is.

His essence was powerful and had a brightness and vibrancy to it I didn't see often. I felt his love and humour embrace me as he delightfully informed me of his reinstated ability to run.

I remembered a discussion I had had with him where I had asked him "If you could do anything right now, what would it be?" "I would run. I would run to the edge of the world, turn around and run back." He had said with a hearty laugh.

Titus was, in his day, a respected runner. With no transport, Hopi men were often out running messages and scouting for land and water throughout the desert.

Titus loved the freedom and adventure of it. His past had not been easy and as many other Native people in many countries could probably relate, he was taken from his family as a young man and raised in a Christian household far away.

Forbidden to see or have anything to do with his family for many years, Titus became distraught at hearing of his beloved Mother's illness. Without a second thought he ran away, making the long journey back to his home in Hoteville.

Unfortunately it wasn't in time and his Mother had passed away just before he could get there.

Memories flooded back, filling my heart with the joy of his contagious laughter mixed with beautiful prayerful chants that brought pictures to mind of the ever-present playful twinkle in his eye.

"But something very special happened as well." Rosa's voice almost sounded excited. "Do you know about the stories of the White Buffalo Woman and her promise to the people?"

I acknowledged that I did and she continued.

"Well, the white buffalo has been born!"

This news was fantastic as it signalled the beginning of the time of transformation spoken of in many indigenous prophecies, including the Hopi.

I became quite excited about getting back.

I managed to secure a cleaning job at the pub on top of the bar work, which enabled me to put aside even more money than I had planned.

I now knew I would be able to make it back for my target of the first week in December and made plans to book tickets.

I knew my Mother was disappointed. She had hoped to spend more time with me as we had only seen each other a handful of times during my entire stay at Oxford.

Four months had flown by but I was more than looking forward to moving on. I had a hard time with the constant cold and sleety rain.

The day I landed in London, after coming from two beautiful clear-skied sunsets, down through dense grey clouds as we came in to land, was the last time I had seen blue sky.

What amazed me was that most people held the general thought, when they woke in the morning that it would be another grey day, and believe it or not, it was!

I could feel my connection to England through many past lives, but I also had the awareness I had finished with it.

It was a feeling deep within me that I had had an extensive history there but I had now completed my purpose in that part of the world. I wasn't sad to be leaving. I was however sad to leave my Mother. I decided I would spend my last two weeks there with her.

The following day was standard. Get up at five am to clean the pub, head off for an hour bike ride, another hour of exercises, shower and breakfast, all in time to start the morning bar shift by 10am.

It was tough some mornings considering I worked 'till ten thirty at night, but a part of me thrived on it.

This day however, before lunch at twelve o'clock, I had to make my way upstairs to lie down.

Sleep enveloped me and as soon as my head touched the pillow and I was drawn in to a very deep meditation. It was similar to when the Pleadians had wanted to communicate to me, so I allowed it to lead me.

I was taken in to a forest. It was very dark with only a hint of moonlight coming through the silhouetted pines and aspen.

A noise behind me drew my attention and when I spun around I saw Nancy. Terrified, she was encircled by a group of disturbing creatures. They were moving closer to her, causing her to retreat even further into an enclosure of volcanic rock with no way out.

I acted immediately, calling upon all the strength I had, I moved in with the intention of protecting Nancy.

The last thing I remember was a huge flash of light penetrating the structure of the cells within my body.

I woke up and checked the time as I felt I had been asleep for hours and I was concerned I had missed getting back to work in time. I was relieved to see I had only been out for 20 minutes.

I loved these blasts of energy I received during these out-of-body sessions but what I had just experienced disturbed me as it   felt   too   real.

9 SECOND TIME AROUND

I guess it was inevitable that somewhere along the line I would have a few hiccups, and equally that it might happen in L.A.

This time through the airport my bags were searched and I was interrogated for the best part of three hours, despite this time, having a destination address in Sedona and far more money on hand than my first visit.

Once they released me, one of the officers explained that I just happened to fit the randomly picked description of the day for their focus, to stop drug trafficking.

By the time I got to the Hotel I was truly exhausted so I went straight to my room, deciding to catch up with Nigel the following day.

Two o'clock in the afternoon rolled around before I was able to get up and that was only because the others in the dorm room were talking and laughing, completely oblivious or completely insensitive to me being fast asleep.

"Oh my gosh, I didn't know anyone was there!" One of them squealed when I pulled the blankets and sleeping bag off my body to sit up.

"Sorry if we woke you." The other girl said with an obvious English accent.

"That's OK, I really need to get up anyway." I assured them.

As my eyes began to focus I noticed both girls had to be in their twenties. The one with curly blonde hair was Lisa. She had a surplus of freckles and huge brown doe-like eyes, while Jenny had a more subdued homely look with dark glasses and auburn hair pulled back in what must have been a hurry.

"Do you want to come out for lunch with us?" Lisa asked.

"Sure, where do you think you'll go?" I enquired to make sure we wouldn't wind up at a McDonald's or worse.

"We've been to a really nice restaurant around the corner a few times. Their prices aren't too bad either."

I tidied up, dressed quickly, and followed them out the door into the streets of Venice Beach.

I really enjoyed Venice Beach. It had a Bohemian feel to it.

From the lowliest street person to the wealthiest film star, this area was quite a strange mix of people.

We passed by several artsy stores I vowed to return to later, and what appeared to be a huge metaphysical store caught my eye. I hadn't noticed it the last time I was here.

I soaked up the warmth I had missed terribly.

Lunch was great and the menu provided plenty of vegetarian options although my companions chose cuisine as close to a traditional English dish as they could find.

Jenny was also from England but from an area on the other side of the country to Lisa which was reflected in her accent. They were travelling together and were only in America for a couple of weeks. They were planning on working in L.A., and then heading off to Japan for a couple of months before returning to their jobs in London.

I was just about to ask them about why they were drawn to Japan when I was disrupted by a very loud, screaming and ranting lady who was pushing her way through the restaurant, knocking tables and people as she went.

We quickly moved from her line of fire and she disappeared as quickly as she came.

Left with the unmistakable scent of homelessness, we were given the perfect opportunity to consider the fine line keeping us from being in that very same place in life.

I thanked the Universe for all it had provided, and me for having the courage to listen to the tiny voice within, now becoming stronger every day.

Nigel didn't surface until the following day so I arranged to meet him on the roof that night for a glass of wine while we watched the sunset.

I spent most of the day browsing through papers for a suitable van to buy and the rest in the shop I had spotted the day before.

I could have disappeared in there, never to be found again. I hadn't experienced anything like it. So many different belief systems represented in breathtaking sculptures, paintings and books. Wonderful smells of incense' and jewellery from other lands that reminded me of something familiar yet intangible. With subtle ease I became transported into another time and place while walking through the huge carved wooden doors; themselves resembling something from an Arabian fantasy. I didn't want to leave. I was however, already five minutes late to meet Nigel. Taking my new pack of tarot cards I ran the four blocks back to the hotel.

The night couldn't have been more picturesque. The machines ploughing the beach had just completed their last sweep and the time of day when everything begins to become still, was enfolding us.

It was my favourite part of the day. People start relaxing, nature winds down with birds making their way back to their nests for the night. Such a wonderful calm was present.

As the sun descended beyond the horizon it generated the familiar vibrant orange-red skies I had come to really love about California.

So many people had given L.A a hard time but I loved it. Granted, I never stayed for any great length of time and it had an energy about it as if it was ready to 'snap' at any moment, but there was definitely something dynamic about it, Venice Beach anyway.

Nigel talked of how busy he had been over the last few months and how he had missed me.

He had taken a trip with his young son back to Italy where he was born. He was working incredibly hard to be able to return there with the ability of buying a business to support his family.

Although the job he was doing here caused considerable amounts of stress, his goal was potent enough to keep him going with intense passion.

I filled him in on my plans of finding a vehicle, at which he offered to run me around to see anything that looked worthwhile.

We spent a wonderful night together with a little too much wine, lots of fantastic inspiring conversation and too little sleep.

Regardless of Nigel's pleading, I headed into downtown L.A. for a look around.

I managed to find a bus just a block away and spent the next hour observing the swiftly changing and immensely contrasting environments of the passing suburbs. It was amazing how in the space of what seemed like a few minutes, we went from immaculately manicured gardens, palm trees and villas fit for the most affluent, to small one-storied crumbling adobe looking houses with rubbish, old cars, refrigerators and numerous other household items littering the front yard. Stray dogs picking through the remains of ravaged bags on the sidewalk reflected how these people must have felt about themselves.

I wondered what they thought of each other's respective lifestyles they surely had to pass every day.

I got off the bus at its last stop and wandered to the nearest café where I could observe my surroundings over a cup of coffee.

Albeit being a mere half-block walk, I was approached four times. The first time was to see if I was interested in buying heroin, and three times offering me a green card.

I did need a green card, so arranged to meet the young Hispanic guy at a camera store half way up the road adjacent to where we were standing, in ten minutes. He was going ahead to set it up.

I wasn't sure what I was getting myself into but I didn't feel threatened and was curious as to the procedure of something so illegal and yet so blatant.

I observed police wandering around and more young Hispanic men accosting people in their cars stuck at traffic lights, calling out, "Green cards, you need green card?"

The police presence didn't seem to have a great affect.

On my arrival at the store I was shuttled into the back room by a huge non-English speaking man.

Thick dark curly hair, matted from lack of care, covered his eyes. He was wearing a white singlet, stained with possibly many day's worth of sweat, reminding me of mafia films with Italian mobsters.

In actual fact it probably wasn't too far from that in this environment.

My photo was taken and the one who had arranged the whole thing told me the procedure would take two hours. I wrote down my name for him to put on the card; being careful not to use my own, and told him I would be back at the café in two hours.

The next two hours flew by as I wandered through shop after shop, full of clothes and cheap imports of just about everything imaginable.

I wasn't concerned about the shady looking characters on every corner and alleyway and they didn't appear to be concerned about me. I made a point of talking to as many people as possible and they seemed to appreciate it.

My green card arrived on time and I caught the next bus back to the beach before getting caught in the alternate reality I knew the night would bring to the streets of Venice Beach.

Nigel was glad to see me back and had been getting concerned, telling me he wouldn't dream of going down to the centre of the city alone.

I showed him my new acquisition and he told me how the whole area is full of travellers using these fake green cards for a few months before they headed off to other countries or states.

"I have no intention of using it." I told him. " I just wanted to see what it was all about."

Nigel was shaking his head, telling me I was crazy to take such a big risk just to see what it was about. It was much too big a risk for him to consider.

I didn't really see the big deal.

Nigel brought me the morning paper in bed, along with a freshly brewed cappuccino and cinnamon bagel.

The paper produced a number of promising vehicle leads. Nigel worked out what area of the city they were in and we headed out after lunch to take a look.

There wasn't room for Nigel to have a car at the hotel and I was assured it wasn't somewhere desirable to park anyway.

The buildings were packed-in tight and the few parking spaces behind the building were used for the hotel shuttle and customers.

Whenever Nigel needed to get around, a friend who worked at a rental company gave him the use of a variety of cars for next to nothing. Today was a stunning red convertible, which he wouldn't let me drive.

The first stop was to check out a Chevy van and the one I was most interested in.

It turned out to be what I had hoped for with plenty of room and a bed already built into the back. The only problem was, the owner didn't have all the appropriate paperwork.

Luckily Nigel was with me to make sure it was legitimate and he arranged for the guy to take care of the papers and call me when he had it straightened out.

The next stop turned out to be a flop with the van nothing like it was described in the ad, and not worth the gas spent going to see it.

The days passed easily and I quietly hoped the Chevy would come through as it had been four days already and I was keen to move on.

I got a call from the owner of the Chevy on my sixth day back in America, letting me know the papers had come through and if I was still interested he would drop it off to me.

I decided to go ahead with it, and arranged to meet him outside in an hour.

Making sure Nigel was going to be available to go over the papers, I headed outside to make sure he found the place.

The deal went fine and half an hour later I had my own home on wheels.

Knowing I would be leaving the following day, Nigel arranged to take me out to dinner at one of the nicer restaurants in the area.

I decided I could get used to romance and being treated like a princess.

A beautiful night eating, dancing and walking along the beach left me wondering how different the next phase in my journey would be.

Nigel asked me to stay there with him, and perhaps go into the hospitality business together in Italy. I didn't know what to say.

Initially I was taken by surprise. I searched my heart to gain clarity and realised it wasn't where my purpose was.

My Soul was being called back to my Hopi friends and the mystical lands of the southwest.

Although Nigel was disappointed at my decision, I knew he understood. He could feel the need within me to move on.

Having never driven on the right-hand side of the road or left hand side of a vehicle before, I was needless to say, a little wary heading out onto the roads of L.A.

Nigel gave me easy instructions to the motorway and I began the long journey to Flagstaff.

The roads weren't anywhere near as bad as I had been led to believe. Everything was moving fast and I had to remember the off ramps exited on the opposite side of the road, but as it was at least four lanes all going in the same direction, it was easy to just move along with it.

I took my time once I hit the open road.

This was the first time I had seen the space in between California and Arizona so I pulled off into interesting towns and cafes.

Following one of these stops I received my first good fright. Not even thinking about it, I pulled back on to the road after a pit stop and began heading down the road for at least four miles before I was confronted with an ominous looking truck ahead of me, in my lane, and coming straight for me.

My mind was racing, trying to understand what was happening, but in the nick of time I realised I was driving on the wrong side of the road.

I sent out silent apologies to the truck driver and made a point of being conscious of staying so my side of the van was closest to the middle line.

There wasn't a lot to see on the trip, just as I had been told before my first trip out there by train.

Lots of desert and it looked like I would make it to Flagstaff by about seven pm. I hadn't made any plans but thought I would catch up with Nancy before making my way back to Sedona.

An hour out of Flagstaff I started seeing a lot of snow and ice on the road; something I hadn't even considered until now.

I had no experience driving in the snow and it freaked me out a bit.

I went to slow down but found the accelerator was stuck. I tried using my foot to pull up from underneath but it wouldn't budge. It had been straight driving for such a long time it had been a couple of hours since I had needed to slow down.

Now I was approaching the city and a degree of panic was starting to set in. I reminded myself of the many lessons I had had about controlling time and then I calmly continued, trying to alternate pulling up on the accelerator and down on the brake.

Finally it worked and I slowed down enough to feel comfortable on the slick roads.

Still a little shaken, I pulled over at the next gas station to give Nancy a call but found out she was away for a couple of days to visit her Dad.

Since I didn't want to make the trip down the switchbacks at night in the snow I decided to pull over in a car park to spend the night.

I found a large car park where I could remain over night without looking obvious. I got out to stretch my legs and discovered a supermarket right across the road so I wandered over to find something to eat.

Things became a bit difficult later on that evening when the entire selection of clothes I had with me was not enough to keep me warm.

I tried rubbing my hands and feet, shaking them and trying to contort them to keep the blood pumping, but it became too painful. By the time I realised I was in trouble, I wasn't able to move.

I lay there unable to sleep for the intense pain in my fingers. My toes had gone from pain to not being able to feel them at all.

Another six hours passed before the sun came up and started to thaw things out.

A fresh foot of snow had been dumped overnight so the sight greeting me was beautiful, but it took another two hours before the heat of the day had any effect on my limbs.

I took my time making myself presentable to the world, then made my way to the nearest restaurant for a hot breakfast.

My fingers continued to throb, and the idea of running warm water over them was a mistake as the pain it caused was more than I could tolerate.

I continued with my breakfast hoping it would eventually come right.

After lunch the snow had cleared enough off the roads to make a run for Sedona.

I could have been in a totally different part of the world as I wound my way down the switchbacks. Winter had changed the landscape remarkably, however, when I came to the part of the road where the red rock opens up, there was no mistaking the fact that I was in Sedona.

The snow had a magical effect on the rock formations and Christmas lights and music through the main street set it off beautifully.

David and Debbie were my first stop.

During phone calls to them from England they had told me they had bought a new store on the other end of town, setting up another bagel and coffee shop so I looked for it as I made my way through the busy tourist area.

It wasn't hard to find and they were excited to see me, and shocked at how different I looked.

The weight loss had quite an effect on my appearance, added to the new style of clothes I had bought in England I'm surprised they recognised me at all.

After a brief discussion about my trip and being filled in on the new business and schedule, I made my way to the other side of town where the locals hung out.

Stopping in at the bagel store, I caught up with Tony who had his three-year-old son staying with him.

Tony was dumb-struck when he saw me and I could feel his insecurities eating away at him, convincing him that now there was absolutely no way of any chance with me.

It was a shame because he was such a nice guy; geeky, but sweet. Had he asked, I certainly would have gone out with him, as they are normally the ones who will treat you with decency.

Unable to get a decent conversation out of Tony I drove out to the edge of town, looking for a place to camp that night.

Several of the best spots were totally snowed in so I figured on just heading out at later that night and pulling in wherever I could.

The next couple of days were spent mainly catching up with Bastian, Barry and finally getting through to Nancy.

I was due to start work back at the bagel shop within the next day or so as the person they had helping them out was on their way to Canada.

I asked David if he would mind me doing tarot readings and or portraits from the store, which he replied would be great.

By now I had some decent bedding and had started to gather things from the second- hand store to make life easier, including a cabinet that was perfect for storing pots and plates etc.

I had a small gas camp stove, which I could use for heat if it got really bad. Things had come together nicely and even more so when I became busy doing tarot readings.

It didn't take long for word to spread in such a small town so I was thrilled when people came into the store asking for me.

Nancy made her way down to see me and we got to talk about my experience with her and her attacker while in England.

Nancy explained to me that she was, in fact, surrounded and threatened by vampires.

Everything stopped momentarily while I absorbed this bizarre piece of information.

"I saw you come! Actually, I had called to you for help. I saw you standing off in the distance and then all of a sudden you flew in towards the group with a blazing light. They took off!"

I was still trying to deal with the 'vampire' thing when she finished talking. "How do you know they were vampires?" I asked her.

"This will probably sound a bit weird to you but about four years ago I was taken to a party by a friend, well I thought it was a party anyway. When I got there, there was a group of people all standing round an alter doing some type of ceremony. Anyway I got involved with them for a while and they got pissed with me when I wanted out. Ever since then they have been harassing me.

I know they are vampires because I saw them drinking blood, and I knew about the killing they were doing. It wasn't a game to them, they were serious about it and there are other groups spread out all over the country doing exactly the same.

I tried to get my friend out too but she's right into it. They are able to transform themselves into the creatures trying to get me that night. So thank you! for coming to help me. I knew you would you know."

It was certainly creepy hearing this and yet I believed it. It made me feel as though I had lived such a sheltered life up until then.

"I don't want to go back in to that, it's not nice." She remarked with unpleasant memories reflecting in her expressions.

"That's why I felt so good doing all the land healings, because so many of them were clearing land of cult energies."

Our second coffee was consumed effortlessly and just as I was about to leave, a young man poked his head in the front door, staring at me intently.

A few seconds before, I had seen him walk past the front of the shop looking at me through the large windows.

Once he saw me notice him, he marched straight up to saying, "It was you! I waited for you for ages last night. You said you'd be back."

I had no idea what he was talking about although he did look familiar to me.

"Do you remember coming to get me a week ago in your craft? You said you'd be back in a week to go on another trip."

I tried to assure him it wasn't me despite feeling it very well could have been.

I was learning more about the alternate realities we exist in and during several meditations I had been taken into craft of all sorts and made aware of my life and work within them.

In one existence that was very clear, I was an Ambassador of sorts, and would communicate to many different life forms for one central Council. The absurdity of this man's claims weren't so far fetched to me anymore.

The next few months passed quickly. There weren't any more trips out into the desert to do healing work but I stayed busy with readings.

I had tried to go to a centre just down the street for a reading and healing day but everyone had to be interviewed by the organiser first.

When it was my turn to talk to her she became faint and couldn't breathe. I could see her struggling with it but she was trying to cover it up, so I tuned in to her energy field to discover she was insincere with her motives for the event, and because the energy I was resonating in was Truth, she was affected by it as it was reflected to her.

This event made me much more aware of people's reactions and I found I could tell quite easily when people were hiding something or were perhaps a little misguided.

Saturdays at the store were always pretty quiet with most of the customers stopping in before or after work during the week.

One particular Saturday however, brought a man in for a tarot reading. He didn't look like the typical guy who would request one.

At first glance he looked like a builder or similar, and was probably in his mid forties. The session got off to a bad start when he came off with an attitude similar to a pit bull. 'Prove yourself" reeked from his every pore and I never had any intention of proving what I do.

This reading however, was different somehow. My inner guidance was telling me to continue, so I did.

Throughout the entire reading this man would tell me I was full of it and none of the information was accurate.

I would stop and question as to the accuracy of the information and each time the guidance would tell me it was all right and to continue.

I was totally exhausted at the end of the hour with this man refusing to pay.

I trusted in what I was given and that there must have been some reason for it that I didn't understand.

If anything, it gave me the opportunity to feel with such strong clarity the guidance I did get.

Nancy returned the following day with a friend Liam.

I had noticed him as they were walking up the street. It was hard not to notice him. He wore a large cowboy hat, long brown oilskin coat and had very long brown hair. His features were unique as well in that they were more familiar to Europe than America and yet there were aspects similar to Native American. It looked like he had just stepped out of a western.

We all sat down and talked about general things going on.

I could see Nancy was itching to talk about some of the things we had experienced but they were only able to stay for half an hour.

Liam was a taxi driver and had dropped someone off in town. Nancy had come for the ride but he needed to get back to Flagstaff before his boss worked out he was missing.

I told Nancy I was going to be heading back out to the reservation soon so I would stop in and see her on the way.

They headed off just as the sun was setting.

Coyotes had begun to come out of the desert mountains looking for food. They would wander through the streets at sundown, which to me was one of the most beautiful sights.

They were larger than I thought they would be and with the blazing skies and etched rocks in the background, Sedona was an artist's paradise.

I gave David notice that I would be heading off in two weeks at which he tried offering me a wage to stay.

I told him I might be back but I needed to visit with Rosa and the kids to see how it was going.

That afternoon a lady I had come to know quite well came in with a young man. He had dark hair and chiselled features.

I was immediately attracted to him.

She explained how he had arrived from Canada and was on a bit of a vision quest. She thought I would be a good person for him to talk to.

"Sure. We can get together tonight if you like. I finish here at five so we can meet any time after that."

He responded quickly letting me know that would be fine and he would come here to pick me up.

I felt my knees go weak as they were walking out and Barry gave me a hard time telling me I didn't need to make it so obvious.

That afternoon turned into eternity but I was rewarded when he turned up at four thirty.

"Hi, my name is Gregory."

I realised we weren't introduced earlier. Sharon had simply said 'her friend'.

I wasn't sure how I would be able to continue to work with him there but no sooner had I thought it, David turned up to relieve me for the day.

Gregory said he wanted to stay in the shop for a while as it was a comfortable place and there were plenty of private tables around we could sit at.

I organised some drinks and he began to tell me his story of growing up in the slums of Vancouver and how his Mother had leased him out to all the ladies in the neighbourhood needing a little sexual pleasing. He told me stories of his constant struggle to protect his younger sister from the strange men driving through the neighbourhood snatching up any unsuspecting child in their path.

He had written a book about dreams and a person who entered people's dream state to manipulate their lives.

Greg, as he asked me to call him, wanted me to read it and tell him what I thought. He then began telling me about his 'vision quest' and how he had been drawn to this part of the country.

He wasn't sure what it was all about but he was following it.

I saw his face begin to change as he was talking, with several lines of colour appear on his cheeks, not unlike 'war paint'.

I told him this and he told me that he was part Indian but because mixed relationships weren't accepted at the time of his Great Grandparents, all information about it was kept secret.

Part of his quest was to find out who he was.

After an intense three hours we left the café to end the night.

"Where are you staying? I'll give you a lift if you like." I asked him.

"I hadn't really organised that yet, I just arrived here today."

It was eleven thirty at night and I knew he didn't have any money so I offered to share my space.

Greg and I were inseparable for the next two weeks. We had such a great time together, and lovemaking so breathtaking I wondered if it was even real.

We connected emotionally and on a Soul level. There was nothing that felt impossible when we were together.

It was incredibly strange for me to fall so hard and so fast for anyone. I had always kept my distance with the expectation of it all falling to pieces with me being horribly hurt.

This was very different. I was in it as far as I could get.

There were only a few days left before I had planned on heading back to the reservation so I asked Greg if he wanted to come with me.

He wanted to take some time to make sure he was doing the right thing before making any commitments to me, which I respected.

I organised a day trip and picnic up one of the popular mountains and setting off mid morning, we planned on being back before dark.

Our plans were drastically changed however when a big storm came though, trapping us up the mountain for three days.

We had enough supplies in the van but I knew people would be worried about me.

The time spent there was special.

Greg and I became even closer but he had come to the decision he needed to head south instead of North, where I was going.

I was half expecting it, as it was too good to be true.

That night I wandered away from the van to get a little space when I was overcome with a sense of loss and grief. I knew it was because of Greg but I didn't think it required this much pain. I cried like a baby and amongst the tears and heartache, I became aware that Greg was one with me, that we were of the same soul.

I didn't totally understand what that meant in the grand scheme of things but I knew it to be true.

I also knew I wouldn't see him again.

Friends had worried, and the day I managed to get back, was the day I was due to leave.

I dropped Greg off on the southern most point of town so he could hitchhike easily and I made my way slowly up to Flagstaff.

I didn't have much money but Greg didn't have enough for his next meal and wouldn't take any from me.

I had put some of the cereal he loved so much in his backpack, and snuck a twenty-dollar bill into his pocket as we were kissing goodbye.

I reflected on the strangeness of it as I wound my way up the very slippery switchbacks, made even more difficult by my tear-stained vision.

It was late in the day when I reached Flagstaff so I arranged with Nancy to meet at our favourite restaurant.

I filled her in on my spectacular past two weeks and talked about plans to do more earth work.

I felt a strange numbness on my back and when I looked up at Nancy she was looking over my shoulder through the restaurant windows. I turned in what felt like slow motion. In fact everything at this point felt as though it was ticking over in reversed time.

Staring at us through the window was a tall, skinny, Navajo man, He had no shirt or shoes on, which was insane for the middle of winter and he had the most peculiar look in his eyes I have ever seen.

As he turned to walk away we were brought back in to 'real time'.

"He is a skin-walker." She said.

"Skin-walker, what's that?" I replied.

"They are not good. You don't want to mess with them. He was looking at you like he wanted you. You haven't given anything to anyone of yours have you?"

My heart skipped a few beats as I thought of a small silver ball I had given to Greg, telling him whenever he heard the small bell inside it, I would hear it too and think of him.

"Leigh, have you given anything to anyone, especially Navajos?" She was almost shouting.

"No" I knew this wasn't about Greg.

"Maybe he was just checking things out then." She surmised.

Dinner was great, as it always was there, and after an after-dinner coffee and desert we headed to our vehicles.

"Do you want to stay at my place tonight? I have to work on the mountain anyway so I won't be home until eight."

Nancy ploughed the ski fields on the San Francisco Peaks; quite a brave job for a female, she was so tough.

"That would be…" We had walked around the corner to where my van was parked to find the side door open. I looked around but nothing seemed to be taken.

"Where is your hairbrush?" Nancy asked.

I looked around and found it untouched in the draw.

Maybe they were interrupted. It was starting to feel bizarre.

I followed behind Nancy on the twenty-mile drive to her house in a small community near the ski mountain.

At the eighteen-mile mark we passed the same man as we had seen watching us at the restaurant. Still with no shirt, he was walking through at least a foot and a half of snow.

He physically shouldn't have been able to reach the distance he had.

It gave me the creeps and I was more and more looking forward to curling up in a nice warm bed.

Nancy's golden Labrador, Bo, ran out to greet us and I helped unload some shopping from the back of Nancy's truck.

We were disturbed to hear footprints around us. The snow made a distinctive crunch as it's stepped on and we both felt the noise was coming from the mysterious man.

We quickly got inside and Nancy showed me around the house before heading off to work.

I didn't bother with my intended cup of tea and instead went straight to bed. Sleep, however, was not in the plans of whoever then began to harass me.

I brought Bo into the bedroom with me for support but each time I began to drift off to sleep, all the windows in the house would rattle.

I fought it with all I had and when I got to the point it wouldn't affect me any more, the next time I began to doze, I was brought out of it by my heart pounding uncontrollably.

I couldn't understand it, as I wasn't frightened.

The remainder of the night was a right-off as far as getting sleep went, so as soon as the sun came up I headed out to the reservation with the first stop being Burton the medicine man, to find out what was going on.

"I think I've experienced skin-walkers," I told him. "What are they and what do they want from me?"

He looked slightly concerned and then began to fill me in.

"They are people practicing witchcraft. They go around trying to take the souls of people. Each soul they successfully take, adds years on to their life. The closer the family member or the more important the person, the more years they get. They feed off fear. Our hospitals are full of Navajos mainly, but more and more Hopis are starting to do the same. Sometimes they don't have to take the life of the person if they can drive them insane, usually with lack of sleep. Your man will be back so I'll give you some medicine to keep him away."

"Well I'm going to stop him!" I demanded. "I'm going to face him to let him know he can't do that to me."

"You can't do that!" Burton said.

His wife who had been sitting in the other room now stood and made her way closer to us.

"That's much too risky. You can stay here with us tonight because Carlo is away. There's no one down at the farm."

"That's perfect then." I told him.

Much to Burton and his wife's horror, I made my choice to face this skin-walker.

Burton reluctantly handed me a small pouch containing different medicines, instructed me on their use and I headed off to spend the day preparing for the night.

Burton and I both knew he would be back tonight.

Broken pottery and black obsidian still littered the hills behind Titus' meagre dwelling.

I had spent many hours sitting amongst it on my last trip, inspecting the detail gone in to creating such beautiful work.

I wondered why such large piles had been left.

There were large gouges in some of the soft rock, suggesting the presence of a lot of water. This must have been a thriving settlement at some point and despite its apparent bareness; it must have been covered with trees and plants of which a few, petrified in the desert's harshness, survived.

I wasn't sure up to this point what had happened to Titus, but I saw his grave on this mound, looking down on his home and beloved crops.

His land was his pride and he would now remain there with it. I said a prayer for him and felt the gentle brushing of a hand against my hair; he was here with me.

Just before the sun sank behind the towering second mesa, I took the pouch from my pocket and placing the osha root in my mouth. I sprinkled the sacred cornmeal and ash in a circle around my van and closing all the doors and windows, I climbed onto the bed and waited.

Thinking that maybe I wouldn't be bothered tonight after all, I lay down, preparing to go to sleep when I heard in the distance, an indescribable screeching, not recognisable as either human or animal.

Within seconds the noise had become deafening and was obvious that what I thought would be one, was now at least six of them banging on the sides of my van.

Blood-curdling noise continued to surround me as sharp nails screeched and peeled away paint from my now threatened home.

I prayed for strength and tried to focus on sending intent of not being intimidated by this attack.

It was difficult when I had no idea what was out there.

Burton had mentioned that they were capable of shape shifting, meaning they could have taken on the form of any number of animals.

Just when I thought I felt a sense of strength, my heart began pounding.

I seemed to have absolutely no control over it.

Trying to ignore the animalistic frenzy happening outside, I meditated to take back control of my body's reactions.

I was, to my surprise, shocked when it didn't work, and I began to feel concerned for my safety.

Before panic could set in I was aware of a huge spider above me. It came as energy and moved closer, to finally rest on top of me.

I became smothered with the most secure feeling of safety I had ever felt and quickly drifted into a deep state of relaxation, continuing on into a deep sleep.

The sun woke me as it blasted through my van's rear window.

Before last night, it had been tinted, now it was streaked and torn from a menaced attack.

I stepped outside to see my circle of protection still undisturbed on the ground.

If I didn't have the scratches and dents to show for it, I don't think I would have believed it had actually happened.

I made a cup of tea and sat to contemplate what had occurred.

Taking myself back into the experience, the spider came to memory. I wasn't sure what the spider represented symbolically, but as I was trying to get a feel for it, I remembered Burton was from the spider clan.

Right away I knew it was him that had visited and helped protect me.

"Thank you so much for your presence last night." I thanked Burton, having rushed to see him as soon as I realised.

"You're welcome. It was a big task and when I saw all the others show up, I had to come. You are pretty brave to take them on in the first place."

We had a cup of tea and chatted but Carlo was going to be back in a couple of hours so I made my way back to the farm.

Carlo had a controversial history on the reservation. He had been arrested and removed but had hung on out of devotion to Titus.

Since being on the farm I had spent quite some time talking to him about spiritual basics because of a comment he had made concerning some information he'd been given. I could tell it was not for the good of anyone working with the light so I questioned him about it.

"It was channelled, so it must be from the highest source, right?"

"No" I replied. "The most important thing is being able to discern. Just because it came from 'spirit', does not mean it is from the good."

He seemed genuinely shocked at this prospect. At that he pulled out a couple of stones from a leather bag, telling me he had been asked by some people to bury them on the land. I could tell without holding them that they were not good, and when I did get to see them properly, they had natural etchings on them that appeared quite sinister.

We destroyed the rocks and I tried to encourage Carlo to discern all things around him as he was acting for Titus in a lot of situations and he needed to be aware of the risks involved.

A large black van pulled in to the driveway and made its way up the long bumpy driveway and as it got closer I could see Carlo behind the wheel.

"How are you doing? I didn't know you were back." He said as he gave me a big hug. "You're just in time for my birthday."

"Really, how old are you?"

"Sixty-one this time." I couldn't believe it. Carlo looked nothing like sixty-one. I was impressed.

We spent a couple of hours talking about he events of the last year and he told me how the local Hopi government were coming down hard on him. They didn't want him on their land and I could tell he knew his time was running short there.

Nights were a little more comfortable now that I had the van, and it was a good thing because temperatures dropped dramatically. I enjoyed the mornings irrespective of being a 'night person'. The air was crisp, animals were excited about the day, and everything was new. Every day was a whole new beginning.

I sat in the big, over-used lounge chair in front of the alter; now full of precious items left by people Titus had touched.

Closing my eyes, I drifted into a beautiful meditation, taking me through landscapes of lush green trees, luminescent flowers and magnificent waterfalls.

Suddenly in front me, blocking the views behind stood a magnificent golden eagle, or a man, I couldn't tell straight away.

He had a stunning beak that looked exceptionally strong and powerful. I looked deep into his eyes and felt the presence of someone I knew. Majesty oozed outwards from him and without any words, he disappeared. I assumed he was a katchina of some sort.

I was learning more about katchinas all the time. I had never really known what they were. I had seen people dressed as them at the dances and seen the dolls made from cottonwood trees, but I didn't understand their relevance until recently.

It was explained to me like this.

In western religions there are Saints and Angels. Varied, they have different tasks, and all work together for God. In Hopi ways they are similar to the Saints and Angels and live deep within the San Francisco Peaks.

I had to make a trip in to Flagstaff so I checked to see if Carlo needed anything before making way. I planned on spending the night there to catch up with a few people.

I had met a girl at Macey's one afternoon, who became interested in my journey. She wanted me to stop in and see her so I checked to see if she was home first.

Katherine was a little taller than me; about five foot eight or nine, had long blonde hair and was in a sense, the typical American girl next door. She was studying physiotherapy at University and had very wealthy parents who supported her.

"Hi! How are you? I haven't seen you in ages." She said at seeing me.

We talked for hours, until it was too late for me to check in with anyone else so I camped out on her sofa.

An earache had started to develop right after dinner so the pain had taken a lot of energy from me and I fell asleep pretty hard, fast.

I was woken in the middle of the night by what I thought to be someone standing over me, spitting at the side of my head.

The force of the breath's blow moved my hair, and yet when I looked around, no one was there.

Too tired to deal with it, I drifted back to sleep and peacefully slept until ten the following morning.

I raced around town getting all my shopping done and seeing the rest of the people on my calling list. I couldn't leave town without a Macey's Special either.

Passing Burton's on the way back to the farm, I stopped off to give them some extra vegetables. They were on their way out to see a patient with bad diabetes; something that was rampant on the reservation.

I mentioned to Burton about my experience and he asked if I had had an earache. On confirmation he informed me that it had been a katchina that had blown in my ear, and that was his job; curing earaches.

I realised I hadn't had that earache at all today.

Carlo was in a strange mood when I got back so we sat up talking about his fears of being arrested by the Tribal police. Rosa was trying to help him out but she wasn't able to do too much now that Titus was gone.

Making a pot of Kukicha tea, I stood near the bench in the light of the small stove. I hushed Carlo as I heard singing.

The sound came closer and was the distinctive sound of a katchina singing as he danced past the door. We had come to know this to be an honour above all else, so I sent out 'thank yous' to the Universe and Masau; the Creator.

Now that Titus had gone the crops were starting to suffer. There was no need for it as Carlo tended to them but Titus was faithful to his Creator and I don't think Carlo understood the way of the heart. He tried, but he was too 'mind'.

I had watched him as he decided to do a rain dance to bring badly needed water. All set with one of the rattles Titus had successfully used for many years, Carlo began a prayer.

I saw the clouds above the mesa he was trying to call upon but I knew straight away what he was doing wouldn't work. I could feel it. I knew nothing about rain dances but I did know that the rattle was too heavy and those clouds need gentleness to bring them.

Carlo continued and I watched as the clouds moved closer and closer, and then right over the top and gone.

I understood then it was all about the heart. You can learn many things to achieve much in the world but when it comes to our connection to nature, it all comes from the heart.

What a simple rule to live by, if everybody could get it.

Why spend so much energy trying to work it all out or learn it when it is there, in your heart, all the time. I knew I found trusting in the 'Divine' or God simple, which many have a hard time doing. My life had certainly provided me the path for that.

Not having anything else to put trust into, I was constantly surrendering my life to a greater purpose. I couldn't see what was in front me and for the most part, I didn't care.

Now was important to me. Now, was all I had to work with and if my heart led me to a place, thought or decision now, then all I felt I had the responsibility of, was to listen and act upon it.

My heart was my guide and I didn't believe I had to go through anything or anyone to get to the Source. I could go straight there myself, because it is all connected to my heart. I felt I had fine-tuned it well, so that anything being presented to me would be run through my heart. My body would then react to the thought or suggestion with either being wonderfully excited, or I would feel nauseous or almost claustrophobic.

I didn't say anything to Carlo because he was pretty confident about what he had been taught, I didn't want to intrude in any way, but I did send out a prayer that if it was God's will, please let the crops receive water.

Later that evening before Carlo was about to leave for a meeting in the village, we were talking about the amount of new hostilities around Hoteville and how a few of the Elders had mentioned keeping an eye open for stray or out of place animals, as they had the potential to be shape shifters.

Just then there was a knock at the door. Both Carlo and I jumped as we hadn't heard or seen any car lights coming up the driveway.

In walked a stunning man, towering so that he had to bend down to get through the door without hitting his head.

Long curly dark hair flowed over his shoulders and he looked Native American although not Hopi or Navajo.

"Hi, I'm Jim. I was guided here by a few people who had talked highly of Titus."

"Well you know Titus died almost a year ago don't you?" Carlo asked the stranger.

I could tell Carlo was very unsure about the intruder. "And how did you get here? I didn't see lights."

"In my truck, parked outside." Jim said trying to dispel some of Carlo's hostility.

"I have to leave right now for a meeting so you may want to come back later."

"It's alright Carlo" I said "It'll be fine, I'm sure Jim has come a long way, and you'll be back in an hour or so wont you?"

"Yes" He responded hesitantly.

Jim had come from all the way out in Minnesota. Having spent a period of time travelling around Africa, he then lived with the Lakota Indians in the north.

"Are you Indian?" I asked him.

"I don't know really. I was adopted as a baby and my parents never knew anything about me."

I could see some African resemblance too and understood his interest in connecting something that fit to who he was. I'm sure he may have felt out of place his whole life.

The fire had now sufficiently heated the small room to the point Jim had to take off his shirt. I had to gather all my strength to remain calm in that moment as he was an Adonis, and it had been a long time since I had been physically attracted to anyone.

Jim and I spent quite a bit of time together over the next few weeks, working on the farm and taking time to walk around the abandoned mesas; now only filled with memories.

I introduced him to a few people I had met and Rosa took an instant liking to him. When Vana met him for the first time, she became a giddy teenager I had never seen in her before.

His smile had the ability to brighten anyone's day, a presence I'm sure could calm a hurricane, and a natural charm exuding from his aura that could cause any strong man to become aware of hidden insecurities.

Sunday morning was always a quiet one whereby we would often sit around drinking coffee, talking, and taking in the environment that never seemed to loose it's awe-inspiring impact.

This morning was different however in that the constant squawking of a crow circling above us disturbed our peace.

Knowing full well it wanted something from us, we ignored it, suggesting if it was really important it could come back later.

As if hearing our discussion, it flew off, returning ten minutes later with two others. All three crows now circled above us making such a noise the resident cat and dog became disturbed.

Accepting defeat we got up and followed the persistent racket, for what we thought would be a quick walk just over the ridge behind us.

I was wearing a simple but comfortable ankle length strap dress with no bra, underpants or shoes. Jim was more prepared with shorts and sandals.

Our short trip over the ridge turned into a hike towards the mesa miles away.

Sporadically the crows would disappear, and knowing their reputation to be tricksters, we assumed they were playing with us.

We'd turn around and head back, but no sooner had we done this however; out of nowhere there they all were again, squawking convincingly at us to continue. This continued for hours as we began climbing the sheer cliff face of the mesa. The more we climbed, the more Jim and I both began to feel that perhaps we were being led to find water. It could have however been our overpowering thirst due to dehydration.

The crows returned and began circling an area not far ahead of us. It was awkward to get to as the rocks dropped off in places and it meant hanging on to very soft ledges while manoeuvring through tight spots.

My clothes were absolutely not suited for the day, however we made it and discovered petroglyphs covering a couple of places on the rock face. Neither of us had a clue what they were about but knew they must have been important for the crows to go to so much effort in bringing us all this way.

We discovered a much easier way out, but made sure we could find our way back later.

A group of Elders were called from Hoteville and we led a group of eight back out to the glyphs.

All conversations once we arrived, were in their native language so we had no clue as to what was going on but they did tell us the messages were from the water clan and were very sacred to the people. Until this point, these particular glyphs were unknown to the Elders, who were incredibly grateful to us for revealing them.

Jim and I decided to take a trip back the following day to see what we could gather from the drawings. Our journey was wasted as when we arrived as the glyphs had completely vanished from the rocks. Although we were open to anything happening out here, the reality of it was still hard to grasp.

Our connection strengthened with the more time we spent together. Whenever Jim and I were out driving or walking through the desert, two red-tail hawks always accompanied us.

There was increased tension around the village to do with Carlo and we were constantly being approached by entities both physical and non-physical, with not so good intents. I felt both Jim and I were needed to be on Titus's land to hold the light.

Because of Carlo's inability to discern good from bad, we were being used as a balance and protection. I found myself being drawn in to deep meditations of protection regularly, as visitors claiming to want to help, talked with Carlo.

His female friend had begun visiting a lot more than when Titus was alive. In fact Titus had banned her from his land as she was not pure in any sense of the word. Just being around her would reveal her connection to sinister dark forces.

Personally I don't think she was totally aware of what she was involved with and was being used like a pawn. Her presence on the land was intensely disruptive and I felt my Soul go into overdrive in order to maintain balance for everyone for the duration of her stay. She despised me completely and regularly accused me of sleeping with Carlo. Carlo was totally oblivious to her motives and energy and became weak around her. She reeled him in like a fish on a line.

Rosa and I had been spending more time together and she asked if I could do a tarot reading for her. Her partner had just died and she needed direction.

It was known he had been killed through the use of witchcraft and the experience had left Rosa shaken, as he had died in her bed with her unable to do anything to help.

The reading revealed a change of jobs coming. I saw a huge car park, full of cars, and felt it was a school. I sensed Vana having to travel a long distance to school. Other details confirmed many things happening in her life then. We had to end the reading as the day was running short and I offered to help on a trip in to Flagstaff to pick up groceries and fill up some large water containers from a water station along the way.

Typical clear weather followed us for the busy day and after a chaotic schedule to find everything on Rosa's list, we made our way back just before sunset.

Rosa liked me to drive when I was with her and Vana was exhausted enough to fall asleep in the back seat.

For the most part, the roads are very long and very straight for the entire trip. While we were on one of these straight parts I noticed a car up ahead waiting in its driveway to pull on to the road. It sat for the longest time until we had approached it. Right as I advanced upon it, it pulled on to the road causing me to have to swerve to avoid hitting it side on.

I felt Titus with us at the moment it happened. I felt his hands take the steering wheel and control the vehicle. I could feel his energy surging through my arms, ensuring the safety of his family.

Living in this type of environment made me aware of things around me at all times. It was not uncommon for your life to be in danger constantly, and those odds increased with our associations.

A little shaken but safe, we made it home in time for the wonderful meal Carlo had cooked up.

I was woken before sunrise the following morning by the energetic presence of the magnificent golden eagle I had encountered once before. He told me I must go in to Flagstaff, find Liam who I had met once with Nancy in Sedona and ask him to marry me.

"What!" I thought. "There's no way. How ridiculous."

I had no intention of ever getting married, let alone to a total stranger. I blew it off as a possible psychic attack of some sort and went about the day as normal until around five that evening. "Carlo, I have to take off tomorrow. I'm going in to Flagstaff, to get married."

I had no control over what was coming out of my mouth and could feel within my body that, like it or not, that's what I was to do. I had to surrender. I sent a prayer out, stating that if it were for the higher good and only if it was of the purest light, I would do it.

Having no idea where to even begin looking for Liam I refused to contact Nancy for fear of telling her why. There was no way she would understand it; I didn't understand it.

I sat in the middle of town asking Spirit for assistance.

Something pulled me to a particular apartment complex so I got out and knocked on a door.

"Is there as Liam living here?" I asked the young boy who answered the door.

"No" was all the reply I got before having the door closed abruptly on me.

Feeling no further inspiration there, it was nearly seven pm so I decided to stop in at a popular bar where they might know him. Sure enough the bar tender knew him well, and put a call in to the taxi company requesting a pick up from Liam. I found a quiet, dark booth and sat and waited.

An hour passed before he finally showed up. I could tell he was incredibly nervous and curious as to why I would contact him.

"I just felt I needed to get in touch with you." I explained.

I could hear a voice saying "go on, ask him!" and my mind continued to fight the absurdity of it.

"Will you marry me?" I heard.

It wasn't my voice I heard either.

"Are you kidding?" I said, "You don't even know me."

Liam looked as freaked out by it all as I did.

"I don't need to" He replied.

"OK" I said, putting out a last call to the Universe to call it all off and give me the OK to turn it into some joke.

"Really?" Liam was more shocked that I said yes.

What had I done.

10   A BIZZARE MARRIAGE

I spent quite a bit of time over the next few days thinking, meditating and trying to get some perspective on the strange twist going on.

Sitting on a bench in front of Macey's I decided that if I was going to be staying here for a while, I would like a dog. I put a request out to the Universe stating that if it was for me to have a dog, I would really like to have a wolf.

Five minutes barely passed before a lady walked right in front of me, leading a sickly looking wolf. She pinned up a notice asking for a home to the beautiful creature.

I stopped her, asking about it. The wolf had just had a litter of pups with one of this lady's dogs, and because of the wolf's hierarchal systems, Little Wolf had been attacking the pups Grandmother and had become too difficult to control.

I offered to take Little Wolf from her and arranged to visit her the following day to pick her up. I then went straight to the library to find any information I could about wolves. I wanted to make sure I gave her what I could; I knew she was nothing like a dog.

I met up with Liam at a local hotel where I was able to use the hot tub, and we discussed further the idea of marriage.

"You know, this is about something grander than either of us are aware of and there is something important I need to clear up first. If you agree to this marriage, you will feel as if your life is being torn apart and stripped down to its very core. I don't know why I know this and it's not something I'm saying I'm going to do, it's just what is coming to me in this moment. I do know that it's important you know it and only agree on the basis that you are prepared for it."

I could tell Liam didn't full understand what I was saying and a part of him did not want to understand. Marriage was important to him whereas it didn't mean anything to me.

I knew that was why I had been asked by Spirit or God to do this. I had made the commitment to be available to help people on their journey to enlightenment in whatever way was required.

I picked up Little Wolf the following afternoon, then Liam from his day job at the University.

I needed to contact my Mother and Father to let them know of my plans so we went to Liam's house.

He was boarding at the very apartment I had knocked the door of the day I had tried to find him. Once inside, the young boy who had previously answered the door looked sheepish and quickly retreated into another room.

Little Wolf was very timid so I coaxed her inside with us.

I was upstairs on the phone to my Father when Liam bolted up the stairs saying something about Little Wolf and "out". Ending the conversation with my father abruptly, I discovered he had let Little Wolf out and she had gone.

Next thing I knew Liam had disappeared after her. I knew there was no way he was going to be able to catch her so I called Fiona, who had given Little Wolf to me, to let her know she would probably be getting a visitor soon. Sure enough, I was able to pick Little Wolf up an hour later when she had returned to her pups.

Most of them had been given out with only a couple remaining.

Living arrangements were awkward now with Liam and an eighty-pound wolf to house in my van, but we made do. We needed to find a house though, now that we had decided to go through with the marriage, so we asked around.

Fiona came through again with a contact and property that was perfect. Unfortunately, we only stayed a short time as the owners decided to sell it.

I didn't mind too much as it was on a large flat open area and the poor fencing meant that Little Wolf escaped often, making life difficult for everyone.

I made regular trips out to the reservation with Nancy and on returning one of these times, I could feel the essence of another woman in the house. I asked Liam about it but true to an egotistic or perhaps frightened nature, he denied it and only ended up confessing because I knew it in my heart without a doubt someone else had been there.

He told me how a girl from the bar had driven him home because he was too drunk and nothing had happened. I believed him that nothing happened but I was disappointed in that I don't think that was his intent. He was a bit freaked out that I even knew she was there.

We found a trailer to rent further out of town. The price was right but it was horribly run-down. Not even a month ago I had said "No matter what, I am never going to live in a trailer."

I decided at that moment to never say never again.

It took months and many trips to the dump to clean it up.

The previous tenants had left everything, as if going out for dinner and not coming back. Along with regular household things, there was years worth of garbage piled up outside and forgotten.

Two trailers surrounded the one we were in that were similar but in much worse condition.

I found cult materials along with human bones in an ornately carved wooden box during one of my cleaning sessions.

I called Nancy out and we set up to do a Blessing and Clearing.

Liam had gone away for a couple of days so we had plenty of space to work. Candles were placed right around the perimeter of the trailer and I followed with some sacred corn I had been gifted by a Hopi Elder. We stood on the front porch and called upon the light to Bless this space.

From out of the Juniper trees around the property came shrieks of terror. All we could see were the reflections of eyes peering at us. The trees were shaking and we were blasted with bitter cold air for a chaotic period of about five minutes.

It all eventually died down and we could feel the darker energies moving away. We commanded that they never return and this property to now be a Holy place where only the Light may enter.

Smudging to finish off the cleansing, we let Little Wolf out in to the yard of our new home.

Our healing work was being called upon again so Nancy, myself, Little Wolf and her dog Bo, made regular trips around the area.

We found we went up the San Francisco Peaks a lot. There was a cave up there that called to us often. But with the healing, came the harassment.

Black helicopters began 'buzzing' my home as if to let me know they knew what we were doing. I didn't care, it was more of an annoyance as I knew the Light forces were much more powerful than any other.

I paid attention to the crows because they would circle over the house squawking when someone was making their way down my driveway, and I trusted them to alert me of any danger.

I was guided out to do healing of some land around my home and would make a day of it, taking along a mongrel puppy I had bought to keep Little Wolf company.

The three of us spent the day at the river nearby, playing, swimming and healing blocked energy points.

On our half hour walk out I noticed a long black sedan pull forward onto the small dirt road near us.

Before I had a chance to think about it, wheels screeched and at the same time I felt a bullet fly past my head, passing through my hair.

I knew that this would happen eventually and would probably increase with the more work I did and the more energy I took in. I guess I was considered a threat to those apposing the light forces and they were willing to get rid of me in any way they could.

But this time they missed.

Liam and I decided not to have a 'wedding' but instead get married in court, as both families weren't able to make it. Mine were in New Zealand and England and Liam's were in Texas.

It was very simple ceremony with one friend being present as a witness and when we arrived back home, after the ceremonial drinks at the local bar, we found Little Wolf had got out and attacked her mother-in-law.

All her pups had gone to new homes but she still went back there every chance she had. I had hoped that getting the puppy would help settle her.

Several days later, Fiona asked me if I would consider taking two of Little Wolf's pups that had been brought back to her as apparently the owners weren't able to handle them.

I agreed to take one, as two would be too much.

Jade was beautiful. Huge, he had to be one hundred pounds and he was still a pup. Quite different to Little Wolf, he was much heavier with a darker coat. He had been traumatised however and was extremely difficult to get near. It looked as though he was beaten and probably while he was tied up.

There was a weird perception about wolves I had learnt in my studying of all the literature I could lay my hands on.

It was thought that they were vicious and it was 'cool' to have a wolf.

As, in a lot of states, it was illegal to have a full-blooded wolf, people would cross them with a dog, usually a husky. A husky and a wolf couldn't be any further from similar. Huskies were working dogs, simple. Wolves were incredibly intelligent and sensitive. An unstable mix was the end result.

Whenever this instability resulted in someone being bitten, the wolf in the mix would get the blame. This behaviour was however far from its nature, as wolves are incredibly loving social creatures and have been known to break up fights due to their aversion to aggression.

Little Wolf was excited to see Jade and I got to see a side of her up to this point hidden. She leaped around him in an excited dance; jumping into the air with all four legs, twisting her body as she landed.

There were new sounds and expressions for me to learn as she displayed her amazing form of communication. I had learnt the many different noises she made, postures and looks and she had become attached to me.

I became aware she needed to know where I was at any given moment, inside or out of the trailer. Once she knew, she would be content.

I began to see the other dog I had bought, Neean, being picked on. I knew the wolves functioned with a different social order than dogs so I had to keep an eye on them to make sure it didn't get out of hand.

Little Wolf had never taken to Liam, always keeping her distance from him. It only took making a mistake once for it never to be forgotten. Jade was already skittish so the fact Liam made Little Wolf nervous didn't help his standing with Jade.

I then began to accumulate cats, eleven of them in the end.

The wolves were always respectful of them and they seemed to know they were out of bounds. Outside was a different story though and I knew what would happen to a cat left in the yard alone with them, so I made sure they stayed well away.

Inside was pleasant; with Little Wolf allowing the kittens to crawl all over her and Jade loved watching them but kept his distance.

Little Wolf revealed more of her character once Jade had arrived and her sense of humour shone through.

She would come inside while I was sitting down watching T.V., coming right up to me and then ever so quickly she would grab a shoe, slipper, book or whatever else was right in front of me and race outside with it.

It then became a game, as she danced around with it proudly in her mouth. This game became more difficult for me when she decided to build a den in the yard, with those items disappearing into its depths.

Little Wolf challenged me one day, but I was prepared for it. I had read a lot about the structure of their units and knew at some point she would challenge me, as she was naturally an Alfa female. It had been concluded that she must have come out of the wild injured as she had a broken tail and some of her teeth had been smashed. Sometimes I noticed her hips giving her problems as well, which could have been old age, but no one really knew.

I kept my cool as she came straight at me. Instead of backing down or being frightened, I lunged at her, opening my mouth to show all my teeth and letting out a growl and loud noise to amplify my message. I chased her.

Grabbing her by the neck, I pushed her to the ground and held her head into the dirt until I felt her body relax. I had won.

I was now the Alfa Bitch.

From then on she respected me and listened when I asked anything of her. I had learned quickly that I had to treat her as if she was another member of the family and not a dog that is used to receiving commands. I could ask something of her and know she would decide if she wanted to do it or not. I had no desire to try to train her.

After a year, Liam had become difficult to be around. He had started drinking a lot and I wondered about drugs. His history had been thick with abuse and experimenting with the dark forces and his opportunity to transform his life was being wasted by his weakness and lack of will power.

I followed my heart with information I was given to share with him and ways of working with the light to help him move through the tough and painful points.

I was working for a local Auto Electrician, which paid for rent and food. Liam still drove a taxi every once in a while and had quit his day job at the university. I was noticing money disappearing from my wallet and assumed he was using this for drugs or alcohol.

Winters were harsh in Flagstaff in some ways. I didn't like the cold at all and driving on ice gave me the creeps but an advantage of living in that area was that despite huge amounts of snow, the days typically had beautiful clear blue skies.

This particular day was no exception. I decided to take the wolves and the dog for a walk in a new area just out of town. I took along some food to cook up and planned on spending the day there.

We had a fantastic time. I always loved the opportunity to let them run free. For the most part I had to keep them on a lead, as they would disappear when they wanted.

Now, they played in the snow for hours, chasing each other around, tumbling through thickets of pine needles and aspen leaves, covered with up to three feet of fresh snow.

I had cooked some rice for lunch and cleared away the mess when I started to feel a very strange energy surround me.

I was overcome with an urgent message to get out of there.

As I turned to call the wolves in I noticed time had slowed down, I felt numb and almost like I had no control over what was happening; it was all being done for me.

The wolves came and jumped into the van straight away.

They had never done that before.

I looked out the window to see a truck pull up next to us in the car park. I closed the side door and made my way up to the driver's seat.

I knew I would only get one opportunity to start the van and it had a habit of requiring two or three in this type of cold.

With everything still in a numb slow motion, I turned the key in the ignition. As the van's frozen engine began turning over slowly I looked up to see in the rear view mirror, a hand coming in through the back window.

The man was fully covered with gloves, hat and a thick snow-worthy jacket, but his eyes were what startled me. They were black and lifeless.

He felt Soul-less, like a zombie.

The van fired up before he could get his hand on the latch and I took off as fast as I could without going in to a spin.

Through my side mirror I saw a second man, still at the truck. He reached in, grabbed a shotgun from the rack on the back of the cab and fired at me twice before I was able to turn into the main road and hurry home.

It took ten miles to reach the nearest gas station before the effects settled in and I began to shake, releasing all the shock.

I knew someone was trying to stop me doing all the earth work and helping out on the reservation to maintain the energies Titus had worked so hard for. I tried to grasp who it was that they were using to do their dirty work as it clearly wasn't human.

I wondered how often I would have to deal with these attacks.

Liam wanted me to report the incident to the police but there was no way they would catch them. I knew it was directed at me, so it wasn't likely to happen to anyone else.

I told Liam I wanted to end the relationship. It had been a year and he had blatantly gone against the agreement we had made before we married and I had had enough.

Liam went crazy; he couldn't handle it and refused to leave. I continued on as best I could, the whole time maintaining the relationship was over.

At the local health food store, I noticed a guy riding by on a huge Harley Davidson, and I knew I would be meeting him soon.

Through a friend of Liam's, I got a job driving a taxi.

I loved it as I got to travel all over the area and the best part was that it paid really well. So well, that I decided to buy a Harley Davidson.

I had always wanted one, and when I saw an old one sitting in the local bike store I knew I needed to get it.

My brother Stuart had now moved to America and was living in Colorado with a girl he met on a flight back to New Zealand. When I told him about the bike, he offered to give me the money to buy it. I jumped at the opportunity and within a couple of days I had it in my back yard.

It needed lots of work; in fact it needed to be totally rebuilt, but I wanted to learn about them and do as much of it as I could.

It was a beautiful old bike. A 1978 Sportster, painted black with a Statute of Liberty sticker on the tank. That was the first thing I vowed to change.

I chose a pearl-white paint colour and decided to make my own saddlebags and accessories from Elk hide, tanned in the traditional Native American way.

I did as much of the mechanical work that I could before taking it back to the store I had bought it from to have it bored-out.

In the mean time, Liam had offered to make the saddlebags for me as he had done some work with leather in the past.

I had a lot to do with the big Harley Davidson shop on the way to Williams and found one of the owners to be very helpful.

I saw him at Macey's one day and was asking him about making up a pack rack for the back of the bike when his friend joined us.

His friend was the guy I had seen on the large bike a couple of months previously.

"Well this is the guy you should be talking to, Lenny's a welder." Monty said as he motioned to this beautiful man in front of me.

"That's me" Lenny replied with a smile that affected me to the very core. I'm sure if I hadn't been sitting down I would have fallen.

I filled Lenny in on what I wanted to do and he said he'd have a look.

I picked them both up the next day and took them out to my house. Lenny had a big grey Newfoundland, which we piled into the back of my truck as well. They stayed long enough to see what I was wanting done to the bike and to have a cup of tea before I had to get Monty back for an appointment.

Dropping Lenny off at his house, I told him if he ever wanted to get together or go out, I would be available. He gave a shy smile and walked away. There was something about his mesmerising blue eyes I felt was familiar.

I saw Lenny a few more times at Macey's, each time having to let him know I was interested in going out with him before he took me seriously.

On our first date, he told me he was hesitant because when he had asked someone about me they had told him I was married to Liam. I told him about our break-up and that it wasn't an issue for me.

That was the beginning of many wonderful dinners around town and I was looking forward to getting the bike finished so we could go riding together.

I joined the gym and would sometimes meet up with Lenny in the spa pool after a workout.

Somehow, each time we got together like that, the conversation wound up being about him and his past.

He had been raised in a cult family. Sexually, mentally and physically abused by his Mother, Lenny was desperately trying to heal that part of his life.

One of the unfortunate things about it was, the members of the cults are brainwashed to kill themselves should they ever try to cut ties.

Each time we met and talked through some of the issues he was dealing with, he would disappear for days and avoid meeting me. It took me a while to find out about the incredible depression he had to deal with. He explained that when we got together he was overwhelmed with the urge to talk about it, but then afterwards the repercussions would kick in.

I sent a lot of healing to him and was aware of his guides talking to him through me, helping to resolve and move on from so much pain.

I started having visions and going in to dream-space with him and realised we were very strongly connected. He felt to be my Soul Mate, my 'true' love on a very deep unconditional level.

My bike was still in the shop and I was having a lot of problems with Liam. He was not moving on and had begun to call Lenny at all hours of the night.

I decided to get away because I had begun to bleed a lot. Not just a heavy period, but continuously for weeks. I knew it was stress so I called Stuart and told him I was on my way for a visit.

Lenny dropped me off at the bus station and I arrived in Boulder the following day.

It was a good trip. It had been a long time since I had seen Stuart, and his new girlfriend, Tammy. She seemed nice enough.

She was into Shamanism and was being taught by a local lady, which I thought was strange for some reason. Along with the huge amounts of money she was paying to do the course, they were starting to have some issues with the ongoing expense of it as the lady continued to put the price up.

Tammy was doing a 'journey' the night I arrived and asked if I would join in.

I didn't understand the practice of Shamanism but sat in while Tammy was taken through what appeared to be a guided meditation. I tuned-in but didn't receive much until I opened my eyes to see a huge elk standing in the room. I felt the essence of a being come to me, telling me she had been holding out for me to have children, but as that was unlikely now, she wanted to ask me if it would be OK for her to come through my brother and Tammy.

I agreed of course and without really thinking about it at the end of the session, I told Stuart and Tammy about it.

Tammy was excited about the elk as it was her totem, and she seemed equally excited about the girl.

A week there was long enough to rest, and the bleeding had subsided, so I headed back to Flagstaff and to a bike that should be ready to ride.

Lenny was waiting at the bus station for me as promised and I was glad to see him. I had missed him, despite us not being heavily involved. It was a close relationship in that we felt comfortable around each other, Lenny could talk to me about things he was unable to tell anyone and I would hold him until he went to sleep at night. It was comfortable, with no pressure.

I knew our connection was spiritual and had a very specific reason.

My bike was ready and perfect timing as it was coming up on Christmas. I wanted to go out riding but the weather wasn't suited for bikes at this time.

I had arranged to meet Lenny to go to the movies but had sat at home waiting for him to pick me up.

After an hour and a half I couldn't believe he had stood me up. That night, before I fell to sleep, I had a vision of him standing in a kitchen. With him, was a lady and a young girl. I knew this was where he was instead of with me, I was so angry.

He caught up with me the next morning before work at Macey's telling me a story about how he couldn't make it.

I then told him where he actually was, describing the room and people in it clearly that I had seen the night before.

He was shaken and called me a witch.

As he quickly got up to leave I said, "There was no reason to lie to me. We're not in a romantic relationship, why couldn't you tell me the truth?"

"I don't know" Was all he could muster before disappearing quickly.

Two weeks passed before I saw him again. He came to my house and told me how he realised he was an idiot. He told me all about the woman he was with and the little girl who had come to think of him as her Father, making it a hard relationship to get out of.

I told him I didn't want any commitments from him and there was no reason we couldn't be friends. This seemed to release him and we spent a lot of time together, just enjoying each other's company and continued intense sessions about the past.

I began to get feelings creep in suggesting it was time for me to leave again.

I felt as though I had just got set up and comfortable.

Jim had come in from the reservation as Carlo had been arrested and he was no longer able to stay on the land.

I checked with my landlord and organised for Jim to move in to the trailer next door.

The landlord had spent a bit of time cleaning and fixing it up so Jim was happy when he found out how cheap it was.

Within a week I knew I had to leave. I had no idea where to but I felt it had to be south; out of the cold as I would be on the motorcycle.

I went and did a two-day motorcycle course in Winslow to feel more confident on the roads as it had been a long time since I had ridden a bike.

Lenny was upset when I told him and I noticed quite a change in the way he acted around me from then on.

I gave my boss a month's notice and started to get things sorted out to leave. Leaving meant I wouldn't be able to take the wolves with me, which was devastating and I had no idea who would be able to take care of them.

I contacted Liam and asked if he wanted to move back into the trailer. He jumped at the opportunity as he had been paying high prices to board with people around town.

"The condition is you have to take the wolves." I told him.

I knew he genuinely cared about animals and would give them what they needed. I hated to do this to them but I had to follow my heart. There was obviously something else important out there for me to do.

I had worked out how much the taxi company had owed me based upon the bond I had paid every day for the car. I hadn't done any damage so I was entitled to get all of it back. When I handed it to the owner four days before I was due to leave, he told me he wasn't going to pay it because Liam owed him some money.

I couldn't believe it. It was all the money I had and I depended on it to be able to leave. I called Liam asking him to sort it out. It was a crazy two days with him still refusing to pay.

I called him up over the open phone so all the drivers in the cabs could hear the call.

"I'm not paying you anything, if you want to do anything about it, take me to court." He sounded so smug.

"OK I will have to then" Was all I could say. I had no way of retrieving this money any other way.

Feeling defeated, I began to look at options other than leaving.

Late that night I received a call from one of the drivers. "What did you do? You must be some powerful witch lady or something."

"Why, what happened?" I asked.

"Right after the boss hung up on you, one of the taxi's transmissions blew up. It went to the shop and as soon as it was back out on the street, another blew. It's been crazy Leigh, it even happened one more time. Gary's has been going crazy. I told him it was because he's doing the dirty on you and karma's coming to bite him on the butt!"

I couldn't believe it but sure enough ten minutes later the owner was on the phone wanting to know how much he owed me.

I gave him the amount I had worked out, and told him he would have to drop it off to me because I had already sold my truck.

"See you in twenty minutes." He said bluntly.

An unfamiliar truck pulled into my driveway half an hour later but I saw George sitting in the passenger seat.

He, along with a large, rough-looking accomplice climbed out of the large GMC. As the second guy stepped out, he made a point of letting me see a gun wrapped in a shirt that he had stuffed into a bag, as he threw it over his shoulder.

I couldn't believe George had felt threatened by me, but I was grateful I was getting paid.

It took all of three minutes for him to hand over the money and me to sign a receipt for it before they left.

It was an incredibly awkward situation and certainly not how I wanted to end anything.

I was quite shocked to see how powerful the energy was in taking care of me which was comforting to feel before my next step. I could feel the full support of the Universe and knew my path was important.

Lenny took me out for dinner and rented a hotel room in town for my last night. It was an enjoyable night; we talked a lot about many things. Lenny was worried about not being able contact me so I promised him that if he ever needed me, all he had to do was think of me and I would call him.

I was nervous about leaving but excited at the same time.

The bike was loaded with my well-travelled backpack and I was about to begin a new chapter in my life.

Liam had promised me he would take care of the divorce as I had bought the papers needed and had gone over the process with him, trusting he would be able to follow through.

I had intense dreams and was visited by the spirit of an Indian Elder.

In meditation she took me underground into a round room. There were three others in there, all women, and a small fire in the middle.

The one who brought me in, spoke of many things to do with cycles. She drew on the dirt, using symbols of animals at each compass direction as she explained to me the cycle I was on.

They told me of a series of events I would experience and their purpose in my life. I was honoured on my journey with each of the old women handing me a gift.

Once outside the underground chamber, an old Indian man greeted me. He led me down a pathway; taking me beyond the realm of consciousness.

11   THE SOUTH CALLS

The road out of Flagstaff was icy so I made my way carefully down the switchbacks to Sedona.

I wanted to say goodbye to a Barry and Bastian. Tony was at the bagel shop but said Barry had started going to another café further down the road and Bastian hadn't been seen around town for months. I had no luck finding Barry so I continued on my way.

The roads cleared of snow quickly and I began to sense what all riders do when they hit the open desert roads.

Such an overwhelming sense of freedom surges through you it almost feels as if you could fly.

On my beautiful iron horse, I was free to fly again.

I remembered as a child having dreams every night of flying. I would run, and once enough momentum had been built up, I would rise up and sour over land, through trees, sweeping down into the water where I would often swim with dolphins, whales or fish, then surface again for more adventures in the sky.

These dreams evolved to jumping off our second story veranda, giving instant lift-off. I would then fly to places where people were in trouble.

Some were stuck in burning buildings, others trapped or in danger. I would have to gather them up and fly them out to safety.

I still felt like I was doing this in a strange way.

People would come in to my life and there were always issues there. I would help them work with those issues, perhaps introduce them to new ways of thinking, and in return I would learn about myself.

I felt as though I was only just beginning to get to know myself.

I rode in to Scottsdale by lunchtime so I pulled over at a small Mexican restaurant tucked amongst a large garden filled with a variety of cacti's, a small water fountain and plenty of bright colours. The food was great. I normally had a bean burrito and rice, without any of the cheese or sour cream and this one didn't let me down.

Lenny had mentioned that the closer I got to the border, the better the burrito.

It was a fantastic day. An invigorating chill cut through the air but clear skies made up for every bit of its bite.

I had a full-face helmet and thick leather chaps but still had a hard time keeping my hands warm after my first experience with the cold in Flagstaff.

Medicine Man Burton said it was a mild case of frostbite and that I had to be careful not to damage the nerve endings any more.

They would get extremely painful at certain temperatures it seemed, and once really cold, the most excruciating part was thawing them back out.

Right now though, my hands were warm from holding a piping hot coffee, and my body had warmed through nicely from the combination of the sun and a good dose of chilli.

Hitting the road again, I continued south on a route decided in the moment.

Signs ahead advised me of a lake and park so I decided to stop there for the night.

Before I could reach the camping area I ran out of gas.

The ranger's office was closed so I had no choice but to sit and wait for someone to come along.

It was at least ninety miles to the nearest gas station, which was as far as I could get on one tank of gas.

The ranger showed up about an hour later and kindly filled my tank up for no charge. He showed me around the park and suggested a spot to put my tent up.

It was a new area, with part of it still under construction.

With no other people around, I picked a spot right next to the waters edge. There were no spots that looked soft so I settled for the smallest pebbles I could find.

The night turned cold very quickly and I had to put on layers of clothes to be able to sleep, and even more on at around four am when the temperature took another dive.

The next few days were spent wandering through little desert towns and taking my time to allow for guidance or inspiration.

My motorcycle had a unique carburettor that required a lot of priming before I could start it.

At gas stations along the way after filling up with gas, I would be priming the bike and would often have men stop to see if they could help me start it. For the first couple of times I explained that I was only priming it, but the more it happened, I decided I might let them do all the hard work. It would give their ego a bolster to think they were helping a poor helpless woman trying to kick-start her bike and it would get the job done nicely for me.

Having just rebuilt the engine, the compression was hard, which meant it was difficult to kick over.

The mechanic who helped me rebuild it had given me the option of installing an electric start, but I wanted to keep it as original as possible.

Along one of the long straight roads I saw a lot of traffic ahead of me and as I got closer I passed a sign telling me I was in Quartzsite.

I began to see that the traffic ahead was motor homes and they had come to a stop on the main road.

Never being one to travel up the centre line, I waited in line with the rest of them.

My bike was having a hard time idling for so long in the heat but we managed to move before it overheated.

The major intersection was jammed with motor homes and from what I could see further up the road, there were hundreds of them.

I made my way slowly through the town and pulled in to small pizza bar/restaurant to see if I could find out about what was going on.

The room was dark and reeked of cigarette smoke and beer-soaked carpet.

A young guy was on stage singing country music and there were about twenty people, interspersed between the bar and tables.

I ordered a coffee, grabbed a local paper from a stand and sat down in front of the stage to find out a little bit about where I was.

The music was good and the paper had plenty of articles about the huge market going on outside.

Every winter 'snowbirds' travelled from all over the country to hang out while the rest of the country was cold.

One article said the normal population was around a thousand, but over these three winter months, over a million would roll in and set up stalls to sell their wares.

I glanced up to see the young performer looking at me. He shot me a gorgeous smile, which I reciprocated.

When he took a break he headed straight for me but was quickly intercepted by a barmaid. They looked quite friendly, so I left.

People and motor homes filled the town and overflowed the gas station.

I met a fellow biker, Mike, while waiting to fill up who gave me directions to a place where I could camp for free, and also filled me in on all the rules and regulations of free camping.

I headed to a campground for the night as it was getting dark, and thought I'd spend the time to find a free camp the next day.

I spent the following day going through the markets and ended the day still not having covered the entire area.

On the way to find a free camp, my backpack began slipping off my bike when one of the bungee cords broke.

I pulled off outside the small pizza place I had stopped at the other day to try to readjust it. Once repaired and back on the road I found the area Mike told me about. It was huge with at least twenty acres packed to the brim.

Some of the motor homes were set up in small communities and many had ornaments set up like small gardens in front.

I recognised Mike's bike parked near a fence and decided to park near him, as he hadn't had any problems leaving things unattended for lengths of time.

Mike told me there were showers in town and entertainment around the clock. A shower sounded like a good idea, I would find them in the morning.

I tried to meditate on my next move and why I felt compelled to stay in this little town. I enjoyed markets but surely I had somewhere important to go.

I didn't get any clarity and drifted off to sleep easily despite the unfamiliar noises around me.

Another beautiful day greeted me as I woke to the sound of Mike starting his bike. I had no idea what the day would hold in store for me but I decided to head into town and get one of the showers Mike had told me about yesterday.

My body was a little stiff from sleeping on the uncomfortable mounds in the ground which I was unable to manoeuvre around effectively.

There were already plenty of people out and about and I thought I might have a bit of a wait for my shower but I was pleasantly surprised to find there were plenty available.

Set up in what looked like horse trailers, these showers were much nicer than I was expecting. Clean, hot and wonderful water pressure.

I found it hard to pull myself away and shut it off, although there was not time limit set.

Afterwards I felt completely refreshed and took my time at the outside sink and mirrors putting on makeup and brushing my hair.

I was really enjoying soaking up the whole experience.

Things were so different here to New Zealand. It was a whole new world really. Different people with different beliefs and customs. Different food and music.

I loved that. Something within me thrived on experiencing these different ways and I found it extremely fascinating.

I began to feel Lenny strongly in my mind so I quickly gathered up my things and headed to the local post office hoping I would find a phone.

Lenny was delighted I had called and a little surprised, as he said he was testing what I had said about thinking about me when he wanted me to call. Not ten minutes prior had he begun thinking he wanted to talk to me.

I felt a sense of relief within him as he realised this might be something he could put some trust in to.

Things were going well for him and it was snowing there in Flagstaff ~ I was very grateful of the desert for that.

He told me how much he missed me and asked if I would meet up with him in Laughlin in a week. I jumped at the opportunity. Laughlin was a casino town I had only been there once with a taxi fare.

Quite often movies were taken from theatre to theatre via taxi as there was no bus service when they needed to get there.

I would do many long-distance trips through the southwest delivering all sorts of items, from movies to leeches.

On my one trip there I had arrived in Laughlin in the early hours of the morning and was enthralled by the impressive lights. I wondered how different it might look during the day.

I wandered back to my bike thinking about my connection with Lenny and what it all meant in the grand scheme of things.

I knew that our time together had allowed him to open up but my work with him was not over. I still felt very drawn to stay in constant contact with him.

I knew a relationship with him wasn't meant to be but I enjoyed being around him.

"Hi" I looked up to see a young man sitting back with his arms folded on top of a beautiful Harley Davidson.

He had a hat on that reminded me of the Aussie outback and with his cut-off sleeves revealing very manly biceps, he peaked my interest.

"G'day" I replied. As I got a little closer I realised it was the guy from the other day that was playing music at the pizza place.

"You must be from Australia." He claimed with that huge grin I recognised.

I chuckled a little, as some 'kiwis' wouldn't like that comparison very much.

There has been an on-going rivalry between the Aussies and Kiwis for a very long time. I don't think it was even something we learnt consciously, it was ingrained in us. It was similar to the Canadian American thing or how some Americans don't like being referred to as a 'yank'.

"Actually no, I'm from New Zealand."

We talked a little, I told him where New Zealand was as he hadn't heard of it at all and we decided to head back to the pizza place for a coffee and talk some more.

Jackson, I discovered, worked at the pizza place whenever he felt like it and would just take tips. The bar would feed him, however the tips were more than I remember ever paying bands at the club back in New Zealand.

"So what brings you out to the desert?" I asked him.

It was an effort to find many people under sixty in this town at this time of the year and I was curious why he had chosen this place.

"I came out to get away. I finished touring the world with a 'big name' entertainer and needed to spend some time finding out who I was. A vision quest in a way. What about yourself?"

I wasn't sure why I had wound up there but I gave him what I had at the risk of sounding weird.

"I'm not sure. I bought this bike, quit my job and headed south. I think I may cross the country to have a look and then head back to New Zealand. I'm just trying to take each day as it comes."

It's always hard to broach the spiritual subjects, you never know how much the other person is open to those sort of things but with Jackson mentioning a vision quest I felt comfortable opening up to him about my spiritual path.

"There's this change going on on the planet right now, well it's been going on for a very long time but we're really seeing it now. It's a really important time for the planet and us. We are evolving into a higher consciousness. I've been doing a lot of work with the earth to help this process, mainly anchoring energy here so then it can be utilized."

He seemed interested so I continued.

"The people who do this work are often called 'lightworkers' and their role is to transform themselves through releasing old conditioning and ways of thought to allow a higher vibration through. Once they are able to absorb a higher frequency it is like a magnet for it. This higher energy comes to them from the higher dimensions and by absorbing it or taking it in it is anchored within the earth and available for everyone else."

"Sounds interesting, I don't understand it but it sounds fascinating" Jackson seemed to be interested and keen to learn more.

"Part of the process of clearing out all the old is realising who we truly are. We are perfect. It's just an illusion that we are anything else. So if you have the intent to be all that you can be, or as aligned with the higher truth, it automatically begins to happen.

Our thoughts are so powerful, people really don't realise that as soon as you think a thought it begins to manifest. I know that my part in it all is to be as true and pure as I can be, which means being able to honestly look at myself ~ even the parts I don't want to see, and then forgive or accept without judgement who I am. At that point I can make a choice about who I really want to be."

I started to feel like I was preaching so I asked Jackson more about him.

He had come to Quartzsite because his Uncle and Aunt came every year. He had only just met them a few weeks ago.

Raised by a solo Dad who had died from cancer two years ago. They had moved around so much when he was growing up, Jackson had never really got to know his extended family.

His Mother had abandoned him when he was a baby and I knew that would have had a huge impact on him.

Despite his outgoing friendly nature I could feel pain behind it all.

Jackson told me of another woman Carol, he had met when he arrived in town who talked of similar things. She even used the same words so he was keen for me to meet her.

I didn't get a good feeling from her however, as Jackson mentioned she had been trying to get him to leave his body at night and to meet up with her.

If she was genuine she wouldn't be telling him to do that without totally protecting himself first and the whole thing felt very manipulated.

She had told him a story of how they were together in his last life when he was killed, but he promised to come back straight away and find her.

She was probably in her late fifties so that was feasible but it still felt controlling. I didn't say anything to Jackson about what I was feeling because everyone has to use his or her own discernment; and he obviously needed to experience that.

When Jackson found out I was sleeping on the ground in my tent he offered the spare bed in his camper. I hesitated at first because I am such a loner and really enjoy my space, so living in such close quarters with someone I don't even really know was not very appealing.

Later that evening however, I felt I needed to do just that.

We drove to my campsite and in the dark packed up my tent. We put all my belongings into the back of his little pick-up truck and headed back to my new temporary home.

It was a beautiful evening. Jackson convinced me that I needed a back massage after sleeping on all of that hard ground and I certainly wasn't going to argue with that kind of offer so we set up the spare bed and I totally relaxed into being pampered for the evening.

We made love, and for the first time during lovemaking I heard music and saw fireworks. I almost laughed when I saw it because it was so cliché, but decided it could spoil the mood.

There was no doubt in my mind that this was a special connection from that moment.

As we lay in each other's arm he told me how he was disappointed that I was gone that first day in the pizza place.

He was in fact coming over to talk to me when intercepted by the barmaid, but was intending to talk with me after.

Apparently the next day when I had to stop and fix the pack on my bike, I stopped right outside the phone he was using.

Trying to end the conversation quickly with the person on the other end wasn't quick enough as the moment he hung up I was riding away.

Even more frustrating for him he said, was when I pulled in to take my shower.

His motor home was parked right at the back of the showers and when he heard me pull in that morning he sat himself outside waiting for me to ride out, thinking he would wave me down.

To his disgust I rode right by him at which point he jumped on his bike and chased me down. Not wanting to totally freak me out he found my bike parked at the post office and decided to wait there for me to come back to it.

I tried to explain to him that I am not one to peer in to people's private spaces – probably because I really like my private space, so I would have been focused everywhere but his living area.

I don't think he believed me though as he said he had got up and was jumping around and "No one could not have seen me!"

He explained that he had a 'rule' whereby if anything happened three times, he would have to take action, so encountering me three times had given him every reason to approach me.

The week flew by and I found myself having to protect Jackson every night from Carol.

She wouldn't meet with me and when I passed her in the street she refused to look at me.

At night I could feel her trying to pull Jackson out of his body and I would have to send protection around him to keep him safe. I didn't say too much to him about this as he said he was on his spiritual journey of learning and really felt there was something more for him, and I didn't want to take away any of his power of discernment. I would just stay in the background and help out quietly while he came to learn about it all.

Things had changed quite quickly with us and our relationship was getting very close.

I was enjoying Jackson's company and was excited about the prospect of travelling across the country with him.

I had to leave though.

I was so comfortable being able to trust what I was given and just act upon it but it is difficult for others to do the same or even understand it. So explaining to Jackson why I had to go just turned out to be a mess, and I felt some animosity towards me about it as I think he thought I wasn't being honest with him.

I had to just let that go though and trust as well.

I decided to go to Laughlin as it would only be a couple of days until I was meant to meet up with Lenny anyway.

I found a nice campground right on the waterfront and took a look around the town.

Lenny arrived a day early and bought me a room in one of the fancy hotels for a couple of nights.

It was great to see him and he was in great spirits.

The second night however I had an overwhelming sense to go back to Jackson.

I told Lenny I had to go which totally confused him, but I assured him I would call him soon and we would meet up again.

It was 1am by the time I made it back to Quartzsite but Jackson wasn't in his motor home.

I saw the candles blaring in Carol's tent, which she had pitched about twenty feet away, and I knew he was in there with her.

I sat on Jackson's bed and went in to a meditation to see what was going on.

I was instantly transported to stand right between them.

I saw I had been transformed into a massive ankh of light.

Carol was using witchcraft on him with spells and potions.

I felt my energy totally encompassing him and forcing her away.

Half an hour later Jackson came back and was very surprised to see me.

I told him I was allowed back which didn't go down well with him at all. He thought I was playing mind games with him.

I could understand why he felt that but there wasn't much I could do about it. By this time I had become aware that he had started to latch on to me, and that had needed to be broken. Simply leaving like that was enough to release that energy.

This was going to be an interesting ride!

Jackson had put the call out when he came to the desert that he wanted to know his path but he didn't realise what he was in for.

12   LOVE IS NOT ENOUGH

Your spiritual path doesn't have to be a difficult one, it simply depends on how honest you are with yourself.

If you have fears and insecurities, that's fine. If you are desiring to become whole or a 'better' person, your path will lead you through a process to get rid of anything preventing that from happening. If however you resist in any way or don't really want to deal with those issues it can become difficult.

I felt Jackson had a lot of issues and I don't think he really wanted to deal with them.

Spirituality was meant to be easy and happen all on its own, was his thoughts. I tried to convey that we actually have to make the choice and then act on those choices, and quite often there are huge leaps of faith required. It wasn't always as easy as he perhaps thought, as the fears do a good job of keeping us in the illusion.

At this point I knew I was here to help Jackson through a major transition in his life. I knew I had to protect him until he came to trust his inner guidance and discernment.

I also knew I was in for a journey as well.

We spent the next month hanging around Quartzsite.

We would take bike trips around the area and we would meet up with Jackson's Uncle and Aunt when they went to Laughlin.

I met Lenny a couple of times in Laughlin and felt he was coming to deal with a lot of his issues.

On Valentine's Day Jackson wrote me a song called 'Valentine'. This was the first song that had been written about me that I was aware of and it was beautiful.

I had no idea he felt the way he expressed in the song, as he tended not to open up too much about those things.

I was very touched.

A part of me resisted the relationship because I felt at any time I could be required to leave. I was definitely falling for this guy. He treated me like a princess although I struggled, wanting to hold on to my independence.

I'm not sure whether this independence came from being Sagittarian or having to fend for myself as a child, or perhaps it was a blend of the two.

From a young age my brothers and I had to prepare our own lunches for school and quite often prepare dinner when we got home.

Then there was the chopping firewood, dishes, mowing lawns, vacuuming, cleaning and a variety of other chores.

I know we had to do more than other kids at the time but we didn't seem to suffer because of it.

Maybe the independence came from having two brothers. Both of them would gang up on me and blame me for things they had done. I was never believed when I told my Mother the truth and the punishment was always given to me.

This made me retreat more and more often into my bedroom where it was peaceful.

I would push my piano up against the door so no one could enter, and I could then talk to my 'friends' in peace.

I realised, as I thought of how Jackson pampered me, how much I had wanted that kind of attention from my Mother when I was a child.

At a very young age I remember being punished for something one of my brothers had done. I ran in a rage to the kitchen, grabbed a kitchen knife and ran screaming past my Mother on the way back to my room, demanding to hear from her that she cared about me. If she didn't, I was going to cut my wrists.

Despite my pleading I never did hear those words.

Where do you even get those ideas as a young child? We didn't watch that much TV and I don't think they were even putting anything on it that would suggest killing yourself, let alone how.

I really just wanted to be held by my Mother, to feel safe and cared for.

I had learnt that sex was how you express your love.

As I moved along my spiritual path, memories began to surface as I was ready to deal with them. There was so much of my childhood I simply couldn't remember.

One of these memories I had stored away was of my Grandfather molesting me.

The memories weren't pleasant and at first I didn't want to believe it, however it all made sense.

All those blurred memories of that time, the inability to walk up and talk to him whenever I saw him years later and the promiscuity as a young girl was another clue.

I had a hard time accepting the fact I had been molested but I knew it was true. The fact my Mother had experienced it solidified it.

Once I accepted it I found the memories became clearer and I spent quite a bit of time allowing myself to release the pain associated with it.

I struggled with why my Mother would send me to stay with him knowing he had done the same to her. Had she just done the same as her Mother and looked the other way?

I felt rejected in relationships if my partner didn't want sex with me.

As a young child I had trusted this man I knew to be my Grandfather and believed what he was doing was because he loved me despite the threats he gave me should I tell anyone about it.

As a very confused teenager, I caused a lot of problems for my parents. I didn't understand what was going on, I just never felt totally loved. I battled to find meaning in life and my questions were often irritating to those being questioned. Often I was simply ignored.

Reoccurring nightmares haunted me of opening the lounge room door to see a head on the floor looking up at me. It was alive and I would turn to scream for help to the whole family who were in the room, but no sound would come out of my mouth. I felt helpless.

As I watched Jackson string his guitar for that night's show I was aware I was allowing myself to get close to him and open my heart like I had never done before. It felt good.

I found we spent many hours talking about spiritual values.

Jackson would ask lots of questions about what I believed and I felt energised sharing with him. I noticed however a few times how some of the things I had said were relayed back to me in a totally different way. A lot of the time I couldn't even see how it could have been interpreted that way but I understood you hear what you want to hear so I did my best to clarify it and then let it go.

I had received word that my Mother wasn't doing very well so I tried to get hold of her.

She was no longer at home and my only contact was with my older brother.

Strangely, he wouldn't give me the number to get hold of her and told me she wasn't allowed phone calls in her hospital room. I felt that wasn't true and didn't understand why Stuart would do that to me.

I called him everyday and despite him being in contact with Peter, he continued to tell me there was no way I could talk to either of them.

I tried to find out what hospital she was at but he wouldn't even pass on that information, claiming he didn't know.

I had to let it go and I tried to connect with here on the spiritual level instead.

Jackson and I decided it was time to move on and thought we'd head to Laughlin before heading out to Nashville.

He had received a phone call from some writers out there that wanted to do some song-writing work with him.

Although I had no interest in going to a city, I thought the trip across country would be fun.

The last night performing at the bar with the band was great.

I felt Carol's energy had become pretty nasty however, and as she worked in the kitchen at the bar, I warned Jackson away from eating anything she had cooked.

At the end of the night a big cake she had baked was brought out as a going away gift for him.

I was glad he took me seriously about the food and stayed away, as the entire band got quite sick.

We said our goodbyes and headed for the casinos and hot tubs the following morning!

I enjoyed Laughlin. I wasn't a gambler, but there was something nice about the place. It may have been the incredible duality when you look out and see the barren desert and then see the Little Colorado River racing right through the centre of it.

How the desert can be so unbearably hot outside, yet the river is almost too cold too swim in was fascinating.

I liked the hot tubs and cheap buffets.

I liked the lights at night and the smell when there was moisture in the air. The stillness of the nights and the vibrant sunrises and sunsets were unlike any I have seen anywhere else.

I loved the howl of the coyote and the hiss of the rattlesnake's tail. I loved the desert, every bit about it.

There was a true sense of freedom here.

The second night at the hotel I got a phone call to say my Mother had died. I was told that she had gone downhill fast with this Mexican treatment process – not because it didn't work but because the ones administering it didn't know enough about it and ended up giving her the wrong treatment.

I felt however, it was because it was her time to go.

After spending time with her when I was over in England, I felt that she didn't have the will or desire to live.

The next morning we drove to a couple's house that played in the band with Jackson.

Bill and Mary lived in Kingman and had invited us to stay with them for a couple of days before we left.

I was a mess and not really wanting to be around anyone but agreed to go anyway.

When Bill found out what had happened, he called his Father who was a Preacher to see if he could comfort me in some way with the scriptures. I assured them I didn't need that and that I knew about the whole death process but I just needed to grieve.

It was a new experience for me. Up until that point I didn't realise that grieving was a physical reaction that the body had to go through. I felt fine with her dying but my body needed to release.

I felt I was releasing a part of her from within me.

Unconcerned with the high volume of rattle snakes in the area I wandered out into the desert and found a place to sit and weep. As the wailing stilled, I felt the presence of my Mother with me and I heard her say "I Love You Leigh."
For the first time I could feel she meant it.

The journey across the country was a blast. We tried to keep to about an eight hour driving day so we could always see the countryside. I had no idea it was so different state to state.

Travelling in a motor home gave us the extra luxury of having a R.T. We had it on the open channel to hear road conditions etc. and I found the truckers very humorous to listen to.
Jackson had to translate the real southern accents to me as they were totally indecipherable to my ears.

We discovered that the Winslow truck stop had a hot tub ~ that would come in handy I thought.

I fell in love with the road. I loved the truck stop life and the hum of fifty engines to put you to sleep at night.
Some of the truck stops were like little towns, with gas, food, banks, gift shops, laundries, showers, game rooms and places to plug your laptop in to keep in touch with family.

Jackson and I took turns driving and we created a bit of attention driving down the road towing a truck with two Harleys on the back of that and bicycles strapped to the back of the camper.
We overheard a trucker talking on the RT to one of his buddies about us
"If their camper brakes down they can get in their truck. If that breaks down they can get on their bikes and if the bikes breaks down they can peddle their bicycles!"
He got quite a kick out of it.
We were prepared for anything. So much for riding my bike across the country though.

It was coming in to winter and I had no idea Texas was so cold. We were travelling along 40 so we went through Amarillo.

I thought Texas was hot but we discovered Amarillo was colder that Alaska the night we rolled through.

A blizzard hit and we decided to stay put rather that try to attempt driving through it and it was the coldest I'd been in a while.

Nashville looked like a nice place, a city, but a nice city.

Not really knowing where we would stay, we found a campground and checked in for a few days.

After talking to the manager we worked out a trade where we would work four hours a day in return for our site.

The idea was fine by me but when I found myself cleaning toilets everyday the place lost its appeal and made staying in the city more unbearable.

To make matters worse Jackson had not told me beforehand of the extent of work he was planning to do there.

I thought it was going to be a short stop and then move on, but I quickly learnt he was planning a three-month stay.

I felt a bit duped at that point but cared about him enough to hang around.

It was a very long three months. Not only were the campground cleaning arduous but Jackson and I had started to have problems. It seemed so much of what I was saying was being taken out of context and somehow twisted and used against me.

I knew a lot of what I was sharing was because he had asked for it but the unveiling process has a very direct way of working.

I would find that I would begin to ask Jackson questions and that's when it all turned to custard. He felt as though I was attacking him and yet, I could feel what was going on was something wanted him to look at himself.

I would quite often not even be a part of these conversations. I felt myself step back out of my body while it was used to create what it needed to.

I was often aware of the plan and the consequences but unable to do anything about it.

I knew when Jackson would react to something I was about to say, but I had to allow whatever it was to come out of my mouth.

Sometimes I would have no recall of the conversation afterwards, and sometimes I could see the bigger picture of why it had to be said.

Without a doubt though, it always created a reaction.

This increasingly became difficult, as I was certainly the messenger that got shot, again and again.

I understood though how it is hard to believe we are anything but our ego or personality at work, and in this case he believed what I was saying was coming from Leigh the personality, the one who wanted to judge, deceive, trick and put him down.

Trying to convey, "Here is the information you asked for – I feel this and this, and that this is inline with purity of spirit" doesn't mean you have to do it or that you even have to believe in the same thing. It simply means it is what I believe.

It happens all the time when people ask for the opinions of others and then turn around and attack those opinions. There is no one truth of those opinions – merely a perspective.

We each have the ability to discern and if it feels right then maybe you want to consider it or learn more about it.

We are all at different places on our journey so we will believe different things. It is all about learning and being open to learn.

Our ego is our biggest challenge. If we can let go of all the fears, judgements and insecurities ~ our lives can rapidly transform and become very, very simple.

If we react to anything it is because we are holding on to a fear about it.

The most effective way of dealing with and releasing that issue is by being willing to look at it. That's the hard part.

Nobody wants to admit they are capable of murder or stealing for example. So many little things we have taken on to keep us so consumed and separated from who we truly are.

We are all capable of murder given the right circumstances.

We are human. Each one of us has that in us. It is a choice though. It doesn't make us a bad person.

We each have a choice in each moment of how we will react or respond to any given opportunity or decision.

The moment is the most valuable thing we have.

In the moment we have everything we could possibly need.

My questions continued to frustrate Jackson but I continued to be compelled to ask them. I could see what it was doing. The questioning was trying to get closer and closer to the truth. It was trying to show Jackson the truth. Asking questions he would never ask of himself.

Unfortunately as it got closer to the truth Jackson felt more and more judged and would become defensive.

I had to step back for a while and let it all smooth out.

Finally we left Nashville and headed for the East coast to an island called Edisto.

Summer wasn't the best time to go there but I was willing if it meant leaving Nashville.

The mountain ranges we went over were beautiful and although we never got to 'Dollywood', it certainly looked like the area you would imagine Dolly Parton to have grown up in.

South Carolina was a whole different story though.

We dropped down to sea level and incredibly humidity.

I saw places that would fit right in to a horror film. The way the moss hung down from the trees gave the eerie feel of being in a different world.

I felt a strange energy as we crossed the bridge to the island. I hadn't felt it before. It wasn't unpleasant but it felt very strong.

We noticed how all the houses had bright window shutters and weather veins on the roofs.

Jackson knew a guy that lived here so we made contact and took him up on his offer to park in his driveway while we stayed there.

It was a small fishing town with a wonderful beach.

Jackson and Dave arranged to do some gigs while we were in town and in discussion we found out that the area is big on voodoo.

The brightly painted window shutters symbolised those with a belief in it and that the colours would keep away any spells.

I realised that was what I felt when we drove in.

I had expected voodoo to be quite a dark energy and one that repulsed me but it wasn't that at all. In that moment I was aware that it is no different to any energy form; you choose how you want to use it.

Perhaps I have been so used to seeing voodoo portrayed when it is not necessarily being used for the highest good.

It was actually no different to what I had experienced out on the Hopi reservation with the Medicine Men and the Skin Walkers or Shape Shifters.

Night came pretty quickly yet the heat remained. I found it difficult being in that kind of heat. I could handle 120 in the shade in Arizona but 70 or 80 out here in the humidity was unbearable.

I didn't get much sleep that first night. Large frogs swarmed the driveway, which made going outside impossible or very squishy, and we were bitten by bugs so small we couldn't see them. We had to have the windows open because of the heat, but the mosquito nets were no match for these invisible leeches.

Dave filled us in the following morning to the fact that these small bugs were called 'no-see-ms' because you can't see'em. They apparently excrete an acid into your skin to make it digestible, which stings like crazy as your skin is being eaten away.

From then on we tried to spend as much time on the beach as possible with the ocean breeze keeping the temperature bearable.

Things weren't getting much better for us as far as the relationship was going so after a month Jackson decided we should head back across the country.

A week later we were back in Arizona and not long after, Jackson informed me he needed to make another trip back to Nashville.

He was only planning on being out there for a couple of weeks so I decided not to go. I wasn't keen on flying and Jackson had decided to go to his first family reunion in Washington on the way with his Uncle and Aunt.

This would be the first time he was meeting a lot of them and I felt it would be better for me to stay back. I didn't want him to feel obliged to take care of me while he was there and miss out on bonding with his family.

I decided instead, to go back to Flagstaff, see if I could get a temporary job for a couple of weeks and hopefully catch up with some friends.

I saw Jackson off the following morning then made my way up to Flagstaff.

The weather was nice and I really enjoyed the ride.

I got hold of Lenny as soon as I arrived in town and he was glad to see me. We arranged to meet that night for dinner and I went out to the Auto electrician to see if he needed any help for the next couple of weeks.

It was perfect timing in fact, as he needed someone to do a lot of deliveries out to the Grand Canyon for some of the large companies he had new contracts with.

Next stop was Jim. I called him instead of going out to his house because I didn't want to upset the wolves by showing up and then leaving again.

He was excited to see me and filled me in on everything that had happened in his world since I'd been gone.

He told me Rosa was now living in Flagstaff and arranged to meet me at her place the following day.

I met Lenny at the local tepinyaki restaurant and we had a wonderful meal and talk.

Things were going wonderfully for him.

He had moved in with Dan and asked me if I was interested in staying at their place while I was in town.

At this point I had nowhere else to stay so I agreed.

They lived just outside of town on the way to Williams in a large trailer home so there was plenty of room for me.

I was shocked to see his dog when I arrived, with a leg missing. Lenny told of how he was missing one day and after extensive searching, found him near the edge of the railway tracks and it looked as though he'd been hit.

They had obviously done all they could to save the leg but he was going to be better off without it.

We fell asleep in each other's arms in the wee hours of the morning as we had done so many times before, and slept well.

Rosa was looking good when I saw her the following day.

I was saddened to hear she had been forced to move in to town for her kids, because she had always wanted to raise them traditionally but wasn't able to.

The schools on the reservation had become too govermentalised and her plans of home schooling were squashed when the education system threatened to arrest her if she refused to send her kids to the reservation schools.

She saw no other option but to move to Flagstaff.

She went back out to the farm in the weekends and kept up the land and the crops.

"Oh my gosh is it really you?" Vana cried as she came in the door.

Throwing down her schoolbag she ran over to me and gave me a big hug.

"I've missed you, where have you been?" she asked.

I filled them in on my journey so far and Vana filled me in on all the changes in her life.

She had begun seeing more spiritually and felt comforted by talking with me about it.

"No one else understands me like you." She would tell me often and I felt honoured to be able to give her some kind of peace with what she was experiencing.

I understood the intense loneliness you can feel when your life has such a spiritual meaning. It's not because people don't care, but because most don't really understand.

I was sad to leave them but I had to get back in to town to meet Lenny. It was interesting to see how everything in the reading I gave her all that time ago, had all eventuated.

The weather was looking grey and threatening and I didn't like riding my bike in the rain. It was unstable enough on dry dirt but rain just added to the danger.

The next couple of days drifted by uneventfully.

I was busy taking engine parts out to the Grand Canyon and spending my evenings with Lenny at the gym and in the hot tub.

Just when we were getting close he pulled away from me completely and I thought it would be best if I found somewhere else to stay.

Rosa had offered a bed the other day when I was around there so I called her and took her up on the offer. She would be heading out to the reservation the following day and wouldn't be back for four days so there would be plenty of room.

I thanked her and arranged to come over that night.

I met with Lenny the night before I left for Kingman and we enjoyed a meal at one of our favourite restaurants.

Although he was still withdrawn, he seemed to want to communicate more than normal.

As I was leaving for the night he stopped me as I was climbing on to my bike, and held me. He told me he loved me and asked me to stay.

He tried to convince me he was ready now for a relationship and in the past he was frightened of me.

"It's too late now" I told him. "I'm with Jackson and I need to be with him"

My heart was crushed as I rode away and could feel the pain Lenny was experiencing and I felt sense of sadness at the realisation of perhaps never being together with Lenny.

I knew it had taken a lot for him to come out and say that to me, it must have been a huge blow to have me respond the way I did. But I knew my heart belonged with Jackson.

Although I was sad to be leaving I was excited to see Jackson again. I had missed him a lot over those two weeks.

He was flying back to San Diego and I arranged to drive out to pick him up from his brother's.

He didn't know I would be there so it was a surprise when he got there and I was waiting in the pool for him.

We had a wonderful reunion and I felt he was happy to see me as well.

I drove for the entire journey back to Arizona a couple of days later in the scorching sun while Jackson drifted in and out of sleep. We didn't have air conditioning so sometimes the air inside the truck was much hotter than outside.

Just outside Boise at around 10pm I had to pull over and make love to Jackson. The stars were clear and bright and everything felt magical.

I discovered a few days later that Jackson had no intentions of continuing the relationship with me.

He thought I'd go back to Flagstaff and stay there.

He had it in his head that Lenny would be the better man for me and that I should go back to him.

I tried to reassure him that I wanted to be with him but at the same time I was stunned he would do something like that without even so much as a word.

With our relationship sorted for the time-being, Jackson said he needed to move back to Nashville to do some serious song writing and that if he didn't do it now, he never would.

He had to give it one last go, as it was a dream of his to make it big in Nashville.

I decided to give it a go as well as it felt important to continue with the relationship.

It seemed that the Higher Purpose was yet again making itself known, as I probably would have walked away at that point otherwise, for me. But I knew it wasn't about me. There was a purpose we had to fulfil together and it hadn't been completed yet.

Part of my end of the deal was that if we were going to be settling down and living in Nashville, I would have to take the wolves with us. Jackson wasn't that thrilled about it but agreed to it to keep me happy.

The trip back to Flagstaff to get the wolves from Liam revealed he hadn't done anything about the divorce and in fact had forgotten about the whole thing.

He seemed strung out on drugs and the trailer looked a mess. I was glad to be taking the wolves out of there.

I walked inside and found the floor covered in bullets, some used, some ready to be. A variety of empty liquor bottles added to the increasingly sad scene. I tried not to think about what had gone on there.

Although the journey across country was difficult with two large dogs and us all competing for room, we decided to take a detour through the major National Parks.

We went up to Yosemite and YellowStone, meeting up with Jackson's Uncle, Aunt and Brother along the way.

I enjoyed the nature, the beautiful landscape and the rich history I could feel throughout the Northwest.

We rode our bikes through South Dakota and up to the impressive Crazy Horse monument.

I got to see Moose for the first time and was impressed at their size.

I remembered a Christmas Eve two years ago when I was driving a young man home in the taxi. It was late at night and there was a fresh two-foot cover of snow, giving it a Christmas storybook feel.

I pulled in to his driveway and was confronted by a massive Elk.

Up until this point I had only really seen them off in the distance, but two feet away they take on a whole new dimension.

This was a big male with a massive rack, and he didn't look like he was interested in going anywhere. I didn't mind so much because I was happy just looking at him. The beauty was overwhelming and I couldn't comprehend how anyone could kill a creature like this.

This thought reminded me of another taxi fare. This time a woman I was taking to work in the early hours of the morning. We passed the Golf course and saw a large herd of Elk grazing on the well-maintained grass. My passenger commented on how beautiful they were, and then finished it off with "I wish I had my shotgun with me."

I just didn't understand it.

I moved forward slowly to let this horse-size creature know I wanted to get past. He gave me a disgusted look and moved a couple of feet to the side so I was able to squeeze past him.

The Moose and Buffalo we saw that day through the Dakotas were no different, and as we sat quietly trying not to disturb them, there was always that one other person who tried to get close enough to smell their breath and would eventually scare them away.

It was the same mentality that we saw continuously as we travelled from place to place.

Visitors would race in, get their photo and race out again, not stopping even long enough to really see what it was they took a photo of and not caring if they disrupted anything on their way to do it.

We became more aware because of it, and tended to spend more time soaking up the experience as we went.

It was a blessing that we observed that nature if only for that awareness it gave us, for now we have memories that are very real and will remain with us.

We arrived just north of Nashville in a small town called Dixon near the end of fall. It was far enough away from the city to feel good and the National park we camped at was overflowing with Aspens and other trees I wasn't familiar with. They produced the most vibrant and stunning colours I had ever seen.

There was plenty of room for the wolves to run and play through the woods and several lakes they could swim in.

Jade was still very skittish and hard to handle sometimes which made it difficult for Jackson.

In a sense I think he felt rejected and had no desire to try to work with Jade to form a bond.

The days were spent looking for a house to rent at a reasonable price as neither of us were working.

Jackson found gigs around town that covered our expenses, but we needed something affordable.

Eventually we settled on a house that was older than we had wanted. It needed a bit of work to tidy it up and would require a fence around it for the wolves but at that point we didn't have a lot of choice. Winter had arrived and with the cold and snow it was no longer reasonable to stay in the park.

Life became a full-on lesson for both of us at that time.

It seemed like what most experience in a lifetime or even two, we were going through in a matter of months.

It took it's toll on our emotions as we battled to stay detached and to not take things personally.

By this time Jackson had formed all sorts of assumptions about me that were untrue and I found I was spending huge amounts of time justifying and explaining things from as far back as the beginning of the relationship.

I continued to ask my Higher Self for guidance and kept getting the same response, "Just be. Live in the moment and allow. Be true to who you know you are, and fear not."

I did begin to see changes. I saw how Jackson was more willing to communicate and look at himself and the conditioning he had accumulated.

I began to notice how much I had opened up to him and how strong I felt the sense of who he truly was, the Jackson beneath all the conditioning and fears.

That inspired me, and when he asked questions about spirituality and ways to improve himself, I jumped at the opportunity to share.

I found it hard to watch him hurt himself through fears and conditioning.

Words would flow from me to open his mind to other ways of doing things or other ways of looking at situations, and he continued to struggle with me telling him. It became a vicious circle in the end. I felt like giving up, but we had so much love for each other and I knew we had chosen to experience this together.

I knew we were close to each other on the Soul level – only very close Souls choose to come and help the other tackle such big issues. It was worth the effort, it had to be.

I could feel him, I knew who he was.

He was an incredible Soul with a powerful purpose, a purpose that will transform many people. But he ultimately had a choice.

The choice to transform himself so he could then help others, or to continue living the illusion of the life he had created.

He was also the mirror for me to look at a lot of things in my life. I was learning so much about who I was.

Each day a new situation would present itself for me to see things in a new way. So much clarity filled me, as I felt empowered by surrendering my ego and being willing to face some of the truths about my life. Ultimately we are all here to help each other. We are all moving through this experience together and in the bigger picture, we are all One ~ all the same.

I was proud of Jackson and what he was dealing with.

I know he had made the choice to 'awaken' when he had gone out to the desert when I met him. I don't know that he consciously realised the ramifications of that choice, but I knew I was there to help him through it.

He had come from a very difficult background. His Father had brainwashed him to believe all women were evil and out to hurt him so he held the constant belief women were deceptive. He had no Mother to counteract that or teach about compassion or tenderness.

His Father taught him how to be a 'Man', but it was all false. I tried to encourage him to be who he was, not to do anything for anyone else, and not to worry about what anybody else thought.

I decided to spend an evening talking to him to try to empower him, to take the focus away from anyone else.

"It is important to connect to your Heart. The Heart is the key to the Soul. If you can tap in to the feelings from the depths of you, you would be able to connect with your Higher Self. The hard part is knowing what is the heart and what is the ego. The ego jumps in so quickly when you are faced with a decision that unless you are aware of each and every moment it is hard to discern. The key is in taking the very first response. If you are faced with a question, be aware of your very first response. This will be your heart. Within milliseconds your ego will jump in and try to convince you of the opposite. The ego feeds on fear and will try to protect you from having to deal with any fears. The way it does that is by keeping you as far away as possible from dealing with any issues."

It seemed like he understood and I felt a calm move through him.

I began drawing again and decided to display my work at a Native American Indian Pow Wow in town the next weekend.

I drew like crazy for the next week and found someone to provide frames at a reasonable price.

I was excited and nervous as I had never shown or sold my work before but as Jackson was very encouraging, I decided to take the risk.

The day before the show I was all ready to go when the weather turned nasty and we started getting severe storm and tornado warnings.

I watched on TV as the tornado tore through northern parts of Tennessee and then started heading our way. I had no idea what to do but felt we needed to do something to prepare.

Jackson showed me how to protect ourselves from flying glass and move to the safest part of the house.

I tried to get the wolves inside and despite an initial resistance, within half an hour they finally succumbed to my pleading.

While the experience was terrifying, I found it exhilarating and fascinating.

I went and stood out on the road, watching the sky turn greener and greener. I felt the incredible energy building around us and I felt energised. I looked around trying to work out why it had gone so quiet when Jackson called me in, saying it was close and that was literally the quiet before the storm.

Within minutes it passed us by, a block away from our house. The sound was amazing and it left me shaking as I watched it roll on further south.

That tornado tore through Nashville and I discovered later that day, took half of the building I was supposed to have my first show in the next day with it.

I wasn't sure if I should take it as an omen or not.

People in the community banded together and managed to patch up the large tin building and we went ahead uninterrupted.

I met an amazing group of people that weekend and was invited to travel around to all the Pow Wows in the area.

Most of the vendors and dancers would travel throughout the surrounding states, selling and competing.

I sold enough pictures that day to feel inspired to continue with it and I felt connected to the Indian culture.

"Will you marry me?" I heard a voice and turned to see a guy walk in to my stall. He was tall and attractive with a huge grin on his face.

"I'm with someone" I told him and after expressing his disappointment he called over a young woman who he introduced as his sister. He told me he felt so drawn to my energy he had to say something.

Craig turned out to be a good friend who also played music so was able to form a friendship with Jackson as well.

There was however a whole lot of friction coming from Jackson towards Craig and when I questioned him about it he told me his Father had told him a Man and Woman can never be 'just friends' so he always felt something else was going on and I must have been deceiving him.

I realised at that point that he must have major issues with Lenny also.

I did my best to assure him I had no desires for anyone else but it was such strong conditioning he held on to it pretty tightly.

I received a call from my brother Stuart. He was buying a house with Tammy and they were moving to New Mexico.

Jackson had almost finished his writing in Nashville and we considered the possibility of buying some land and moving that way as well.

Over the next couple of months we decided to make the trip and go into partnership with Stuart. We would buy the land and they would buy the house.

Little wolf had become quite sick by this time. Age had caught up with her and the injuries she had experienced seemed to make it harder. Her body was no longer functioning properly and it appeared she was in more and more pain. I had to make the heart-wrenching decision to put her down.

I knew she wouldn't be able to handle the trip out to New Mexico so we found a beautiful place to bury her on the land of a friend, who assured us he would take care of her.

I could hardly get out of bed for the next couple of weeks. I felt so bad. I didn't feel I had the right to make that decision yet I had kept her alive longer than she could have possibly done so in the wild. I knew I had done the right thing for her but guilt and sadness filled me.

Jackson couldn't understand why I was so upset, as he had always been taught not to show emotions, in fact don't even have them. He wanted me to just get over it and move on. I however needed to feel it all. I knew if I didn't feel it, I wasn't dealing with or releasing it.

We finally got packed up and a year had passed with winter upon us again.

I wouldn't miss the cold, damp sleet of Tennessee; it reminded me of England in a lot of ways.

The trip was hard and even the road or truck stops weren't able to lift my spirits much.

Little Wolf had visited me in my dreams a few times but I couldn't feel good about it at all. I felt an overwhelming compassion for all animals. Humans have a lot to answer for really.

When we arrived in New Mexico Stuart and Tammy's house hadn't arrived on the temporary site so they stayed with us in the camper. They also had a puppy and Tammy was seven months pregnant; it would be interesting.

There was a bit of work to be done on the lot to get it ready for the trailer house so we did what we could despite the ground being frozen from the cold.

We were at least eight and a half thousand feet up in the Sangre De Christo Mountains.

Eagle Nest is an absolutely beautiful small town on the edge of a lake in the 'Enchanted Circle'.

Even the cold was OK up there. It was dry at least.

Finally the house arrived and we got moved in.

Stuart and Tammy had begun a business with a mortgage company so we thought it would be best if we stayed out of their way as much as possible – they had set up an office in the living room of the house and the spare room was where Tammy would do her Shaman journeys.

Within a couple of months things had turned to custard.

Jackson and I would get called into the living room for a meeting whereby Stuart and Tammy would begin telling us of all the things we had done wrong. It was almost unbelievable to sit and listen to what they were saying.

What was more fascinating was watching Stuart tell Tammy what she thought.

Jackson and I did our best to stay grounded and realise they were merely attacking us because they were dealing with those very issues within themselves.

At one point Tammy had accused me of so many things I had to just laugh and walk out. After a brief break I decided that if all the things she had claimed were true, I wanted to understand in what way, so I went to her room to ask.

I was dedicated to becoming all I could be and the truth was not my enemy.

"Tammy, if I am all the things you said about me then I want to hear the truth of it so I could look at maybe changing. Can you elaborate on the issues you accused me of so I can see the truth please?" I stood there for minutes as she grasped for words.

Before she could turn away I sensed panic in her eyes and I knew she was not able to speak.

"Thanks Tammy, that's what I thought." I said as I made my way back to my room.

I was in the middle of telling Jackson what had happened and that perhaps we should look at moving when Tammy flew into the room.

She yelled at me "My guides have just told me that the reason I wasn't able to say anything is that you have to discover the issues on your own!"

I looked at her with compassion as she turned and left the room.

There were so many dynamics going on. Jackson and I tried to share some awareness's with them about how we are just reflecting their issues right back at them but they didn't want to know.

We sat in amazement during Shaman journey sessions to see Stuart and Tammy competing against each other to prove who was more spiritual.

Things got really uncomfortable and we felt as though we were treading on eggshells constantly.

The energy in the house was almost unbearable.

Jackson and I made a trip down to the city to do some shopping. It was a couple of hours away so we planned on being away for the day. We both sensed something strange before we left but couldn't place it so we left.

On returning we found out Stuart and Tammy had been married and all our feelings fell into place. The whispering we had walked in on and the secretive meetings with people all now made sense.

We asked why they had not included us and they said because we were out of town and it was a spur of the moment thing. I'm not sure if disappointed really captures the feeling at that moment but they were convinced that was the truth and we knew better.

That night Stuart accused me of blaming my Mother for our parent's divorce. It seemed to come out of nowhere but the conversation gradually led me to tell him how hurt I was by an event that happened when we were teenagers.

We had snuck out of the house to go to a party in town.

I was going out with a guy at the time, who had become very possessive but was supposed to be away that weekend.

Someone at the party ran up to me telling me Alan was on his way up the driveway.

I freaked. Not really knowing what to do at that point I went into the closest room to hide.

Stuart was in there on the bed with his girlfriend so I felt safe. I knew if Alan saw me at the party he would get angry.

Alan and I had been going out for a number of months and I had even run away from home to be with him when he went to a town about six hours away.

My parents had called the police, who found me and dragged me back, totally confusing me at the time because it was so obvious to me they didn't want me around.

I had previously taken my Dad's car in the middle of the night to escape, but crashed it on a dirt road. I had been sneaking out at night; so much my Mother had resorted to drugging my dinner with sleeping pills.

I was messed up with nowhere to turn to, no one to help me through this time in my life.

I had a teacher call me in to his office at school who then leaned over the desk to try to kiss me. I was shocked and disgusted and I left immediately, going straight to my Mother for support.

Instead of giving me the support I so desperately needed, she told me he was probably trying to be a Fatherly figure. I couldn't believe she had said that at the time as no part of that was 'Fatherly' to me, but it is so true of her reality, now that I know of the abuse she had suffered.

Someone told Alan where I was and within minutes he had opened the door and was standing in front of me

"What the f*** are you doing here?"

I could see the rage building within him. I felt numb and before I really knew what had happened I had punched him on the nose with a good right hook.

He stood stunned, with blood streaming down his face.

Just before I had the chance to run he turned to my brother
"Sorry Stuart but I'm going to have to hit her"
I thought for sure Stuart would help me out but his words rung in my ears as I felt my world fall apart "Sure, I know man"

I spent the next three days at a friend's house. He had tried to help me, but not before Alan had slammed my head in his car-door, rendering me unconscious.

Stuart became defensive claiming he wasn't responsible because he was drunk. I tried to reason that he was drunk enough to tell Alan to go ahead and hit me. The upside of bringing this up did however stop any further attacks from him.

That night I woke around 2am to the sound of a new born baby crying and thought Tammy had had the baby.
I felt the spirit of the baby and she told me her name was Michaela.
I thought it was strange they hadn't come to wake us since they had asked we take part in the home-birth.
Tammy had wanted me to assist and they asked Jackson to shoot video footage. We were excited at the opportunity but I thought perhaps it had happened so fast or easily it wasn't necessary so I drifted back to sleep.

The following morning we woke to an empty house.
I looked everywhere for a sign of what had happened and thought perhaps something had happened to the baby.
It was a nerve-racking couple of hours before we got a call from Stuart. The birth hadn't gone as expected and they had to be rushed to the hospital to have it.
I was a little surprised she didn't have it at the house but realised I must have sensed the birth instead of hearing it.

Her name was Miranda and she was healthy. I wondered why I had been given a different name during the night but quickly forgot that when Stuart said, "But Tammy doesn't want to come home until you're gone because she feels you will be a bad influence on her."

13   LOVE WAS ENOUGH AFTER ALL

That was pretty much as much as I could take and there was no reason why we should have to deal with that anymore.

Jackson and my relationship was not looking very good right now and we had certainly been strained during the whole stay with Stuart and Tammy. I had reached a point where I was ready to leave Jackson again.

I never felt the support from him I felt a partner should provide. He wouldn't stand up for me; even when he knew I was being picked apart unfairly.

Thinking we just needed to get away on our own, we asked around and were offered a position taking care of an elderly lady's ranch.

We would be responsible for keeping her paddocks clean, take care of her horse, dog and plants while she went away and basically whatever else she needed help with. In return we would get a house and large property.

This was ideal and we jumped at it.

The property bordered a National Forest and at nearly nine thousand feet up we would expect a lot of snow during winter.

This was the best move we could have made.

The lifestyle was what both of us needed and it gave us a chance to spend more time on what we wanted.

Jackson got some gigs around the area and I approached a local art gallery who jumped at taking some of my work.

We thrived and Jade loved the mountains as much as we did. We would walk up the mountain whenever we had the chance; finding new trails and roads each time.

In the winter we would cross-county ski up it.

I cheated a little by tying a rope around my waist and harnessing it to Jade. He seemed to thrive on it so I imagine the bit of Husky he had in him really came out those on days. The only disadvantage was when he got a whiff of an elk or bear and headed full-force into the trees. I often came out with scrapes and bruises but having had a wonderful day.

We hiked up with the mountain with a group to discover all the edible and medicinal plants available, and spent hours in the afternoon throwing a tomahawk into a tree stump.

I was in my element.

I began to be drawn to areas in the forest.

As I was walking I would feel a strong pull, like a magnet, pulling me to a particular area. When I had arrived at the correct place I knew because the uneasy or anticipation feeling in my gut would subside.

It felt like a very magical area in the mountains and I started to hear a lot of stories from locals of cattle mutilations and UFO sightings in the area.

My work there was again, as an anchor for the energy. Sometimes I had no idea what it was doing; other times I knew I was working to release stored or abused energies. Sometimes energy points had to open and other times they needed to be sealed off.

Whatever the Earth required, I would be there to help in any way possible.

I had been so consumed with Jackson over the last year I hadn't done much else in the way of spiritual work. He was my spiritual work and I need to release a lot of stuff before moving on as well. I learnt to trust another person.

I had never fully trusted anyone.

I didn't trust that my parents loved me, I didn't trust there was anyone around that really cared about me.

My Mother had dumped me for a man she hardly knew, my Father had walked out on us and my Brother had stood by and watched as I was beaten close to death.

Jackson challenged all of that. He brought out all my fears and insecurities and he was still there, telling me he loved me.

I felt blessed to be at this point. I felt free of a lot of baggage. I knew was unnecessary.

I was feeling strong and more feminine.

I had struggled with being female my whole life.

I was incredibly clumsy as a child; constantly bumping into things, dropping things, to the point I was told not to do the dishes for a while because I would drop them all.

I didn't want to be here on the planet and it was the Universe's way of trying to get me to acknowledge that I was in fact here, and it was going to hurt until I accepted it.

So I always felt clumsy and the sexual abuse had taken the desire to be feminine away.

I saw how women were abused in advertising and I came to despise it. Why would I want to be a woman if femininity will be abused like that?

I saw how dressing up for a night out attracted men and I could feel the lust behind it all. It wasn't real and I didn't want to be a part of it.

I started to feel safe being a woman with Jackson although I was still a long way from being feminine.

I needed to be strong and I had only seen femininity as weak; I needed to find a balance.

Jackson really enjoyed the lifestyle in the mountains but became very disturbed quickly.

He felt like he was wasting his life and restlessness filled his every moment. Discontented with his life, he began questioning why he even continued playing music.

His Father had wanted him to do it and he did it to please him. His Father was dead now though so he was at a point he felt he needed to discover what is was that he wanted to do for himself.

Saving Jackson any major decisions, I got a call from my Father letting me know he had cancer.

I didn't have to think about it too much before deciding to head back to New Zealand.

I had a very small family anyway but with Stuart over here I felt I needed to be there for my Father and help in any way I could.

Jackson sounded excited at the adventure to a country he didn't even know existed before he met me.

I had been blessed with many experiences with wildlife while staying in New Mexico, from Red Tail Hawks that came directly towards me; sitting on a fence post straight after I had asked him to, to black bears and elk, all prevalent.

I did want to have a close encounter with a bear before I left so I put the request out to the Universe.

I also had to find a home for Jade.

I knew he would have a hard time with that kind of journey and I also was faced with him not being allowed into the country because of the wolf in him.

This was almost as hard as having to put Little Wolf down.

You never knew what the people were really like.

Again I put the request out to the Universe and trusted the right people would come along.

I had begun taking care of a neighbour's dogs when they went away to their winter home in Las Vegas.

It was a twenty-minute walk through the forest to their house and I would often let Jade run loose as most of the time he had to stay penned because of cattle next door to us.

This day however I felt I couldn't take him off the lead, so we made our way slowly through the pine trees.

Jackson's Uncle and Aunt had turned up for a visit but wouldn't be staying long due to the altitude. It was hard on anyone who had heart problems and his Uncle had had a major bypass and was already having trouble breathing after a few hours.

I heard a crack in front of me and peering through the sparsely covered thicket I could see a single elk.

I stopped to watch her for a while as she stood and watched me. Again, the beauty of these animals took my breath away.

The wind must have been headed towards the elk because Jade was clueless. He was busy digging around in the ground; fascinated with all the new smells.

Just as I thought we'd move on, something in my peripheral vision caught my attention. I spun around quickly to see a huge bear behind a tree no more than five feet away.

My mind raced back to what I had been told about looking a bear straight in the eyes or not. I couldn't remember and it didn't seem to matter anyway. I was compelled to stare into those eyes.

His eyes were filled with majesty and wisdom. He stared straight back at me, looking deeply into my being. I knew he could feel I was no threat to him and so we stood in a state of awe of each other for what seemed an eternity.

I resisted the temptation of going up to him to give him a hug, thinking he may not feel the same way but the connection we made was a gift I will never forget.

I thanked the Universe for providing and sent out a blessing to the bear as he now slowly wandered off into the dense bush.

Looking down I realised Jade was still busy with his patch of the ground and I smiled at the Divine way things can happen.

I had never seen a bear that big in the wild.

His coat was thick and what they call cinnamon coloured.

I truly felt honoured and quickly called Jackson on the walkie-talkie I carried in case I ever had an emergency to tell him what had happened

A couple turned up in response to an ad I had placed to take Jade.

They seemed nice but I wanted to get to know them over the next couple of weeks to be sure they would be right so I arranged to visit their home and set up days and times for them to take Jade to get to know them.

Three weeks later they were still keen and as they had another wolf hybrid as well as two dogs, I felt they would be the best option. I then cried until we left.

Just before we left for LA I called Jenny; letting her know I was on my way back.

"You know before you left you said you'd be back by 2000?" I was shocked for a moment because I didn't recall saying that at all and here we were approaching the end of 2000.

I guess my Higher Self knew it all along.

Most of our possessions were going to be shipped to New Zealand with the remainder being sold at a garage sale.

We then had the task of loading it all into a truck and making our way across to L.A.

Thirty miles out I began having problems with my truck and eventually had to leave it for a friend to pick up and see if he could sell it. We were hoping on selling it out in L.A. but it wasn't going to make it.

We had decided to visit Disneyland and Sea World before we left so once we had dropped off the boxes at the shipping company we made our way to the nearest hotel to Disneyland.

It was early in the morning and the gates to the famous theme park weren't due to open for another half an hour so we thought we'd at least buy the tickets and have a look around the area.

We got up to the gates and I started feeling incredibly sick.

My legs went weak, my eyes felt like they wanted to roll back into my head and my whole body was buzzing with energy.

I told Jackson I would have to leave for a while to get grounded.

Straight across the road was a restaurant so we made our way over and ordered some food and coffee.

I sat and tuned in to get an idea of what had happened.

A strong pulsing energy appeared and I could feel it was coming from inside Disneyland.

It has been well talked about, the fact that music is played there with subliminal messages that tell you that it is the greatest or happiest place on the planet and I certainly felt it had something to do with that.

It took quite a lot of work to balance myself out again and Jackson became increasingly upset. He couldn't understand what I was experiencing and he then became angry saying, "If that's what happens when you become spiritually sensitive, I'd rather not."

I would rather know what I was going into and have the option of putting up protection, instead of being oblivious to it, so I am grateful I am sensitive enough to feel a potential danger.

Half an hour later I was fully grounded and aligned enough to be able to go back into that energy. We spent most of the day there, although Jackson didn't seem to enjoy himself.

Sea World was a lot of fun the following day, until I was hauled down in front of a huge audience to do the hula with a clown.

It was a scorching hot day in San Diego so we headed back to Jackson's brother's house for a swim in the pool.

I was a little apprehensive about the trip, I wasn't sure if I was ready to go back to New Zealand and I wasn't sure if Jackson really wanted to go.

I had learnt he had a hard time saying no; often opting for the less confrontational option regardless of how he really felt about it.

I had tried discouraging this as it caused so many resentment issues later, however, he assured me he was excited about going and had no strong ties to America now that his Dad wasn't alive.

The flight back was a breeze and despite a little turbulence it was enjoyable.

About two hours out of New Zealand I felt an overwhelming emotion. Tears streamed down my face as I grappled with what had come over me. I became aware of a strong connection to the land and realised I was in fact feeling New Zealand and her energy field ~ I knew I was home.

We landed in Auckland on a drizzling spring day in September 2000.

It was good to see Dad there to greet us, and despite seven years passed and cancer, he looked well.

We drove to my younger brother's house in the city where we would be staying, and waited for him and his new fiancée to arrive home.

It was great to catch up with them as it had been eight or nine years since I had seen my brother.

We decided the first task was to find a car so at least we were mobile and then look at finding somewhere to live.

We found a great little car a couple of days later and instead of settling down straight away I suggested to Jackson that we take a trip up north so at least he would get the chance to see some of the country before we get caught up in things.

There is nothing better than travelling around New Zealand.

I enjoyed America but there is definitely something special about this little country.

I introduced Jackson to Tane Mahuta; an ancient kauri tree on the north west coast of the North Island.

Tane Mahuta was part of the original stories of the creation of the land and came between his mother and father; sky and earth, to create the space for the light for us to survive.

We went right up to the tip of the island where the Maori believe the spirits go before returning to their homeland.

Despite having no Maori understanding I felt a strong connection with it.

Living with Warren and his family had introduced me to it in a small way because they didn't live traditionally, even the children didn't speak the language.

Warren's mother would talk to me about some of her dreams, which were filled with the richness of their culture.

I found it was easy for me to understand.

In my rebel teenage days of sneaking out of the house to go to parties I would have to find my way through the bush before getting to the main road and bicycling in to town.

I noticed there was a Morepork (NZ owl) following me the first night. I didn't think too much of it until it stayed with me the entire trip right to the edge of town and was still waiting there for my return.

On one of these nights I bumped into someone outside my bedroom. Being pitch-black I couldn't see who it was but I knew it had to be a man because of the sheer size of his body.

He turned to run, so I figured he wasn't supposed to be there. Instinct kicked in and I found myself chasing him.

At some point he must have changed his mind and turned on me. I felt his huge frame threatening me as he lifted his arms to strike at me, but my Morepork flew down, swooping on this person until he turned and ran.

The Morepork is special to the Maori and it is believed that once they pass over, they take the form of a bird.

Once back in Auckland we found a house to rent just north of the city on a beautiful peninsular called the Hibiscus Coast.

Our container-load of stuff arrived safely at the docks and I spent the next few weeks taking my father in to the hospital for radiation treatment.

I wasn't a believer in radiation or chemo but he felt that was the way he needed to go.

I offered to do some healing, which worked out well.

Instead of trying to focus on healing the cancer, I worked on providing protection for the rest of the body from the radiation and to aid the whole treatment process.

I had done the same for Nancy's Mother in Flagstaff and was amazed at how well it prevented the nausea and other symptoms, even allowing her hair to grow back rapidly.

I set up the spare room in the house to do healings from, and since I never charged for my healings, decided to help out with the rent by doing a massage course at the local Ashram and adding that to my services available.

I met a lovely Maori lady there whom I gave my business card to at the end of the course.

We had hit it off immediately and talked extensively about the healing work we each did. She told me about a Maori temple south of Auckland where the Maori spiritual masters were trained, and how it was believed to be connected to Egypt.

I was excited about the prospect of visiting this temple and asked her to call me next week to set up a weekend that would suit us both to go.

Agnes looked at the card I had just handed her and couldn't hide her surprise.

I had used some of the portraits I had drawn as images on my business cards. The one I gave her was of a Maori woman I had drawn in 1998.

I wasn't sure at the time why I had drawn it and why it was the only original portrait I had brought back from America but Agnes proceeded to tell me that it was a picture of her grandmother and how she had put a call out to the Universe for a picture her in 1998 which was the very year I had drawn it.

Again the pieces all fell together perfectly.

The next time I met with Agnes I gifted her the portrait. She was overwhelmed and it was obvious how important it was to her.

The following weekend we headed down to Te Meringa. My father, Jackson and I followed in a car behind Agnes and Daphnie. We would meet John Boy just outside of Bennydale whereby he would take us to his land.

We planned on spending the night there after having a good look around.

Just as we approached the dam I felt an incredible pull. It was so strong I felt as though if I got out of the car, this energy would pull me straight to the temple.

John Boy was adorable; full of laughter and light. After meeting him at the local store we made our way to his land and all of us felt a wonderful bond with the area.

It was a little cold but we wrapped up and headed straight for the temple. It had been burnt down a long time ago but the foundations were still there.

Each taking a place on the ground in the main temple area, we sat and absorbed the energies. John Boy explained how they had discovered the layout of the buildings on the site was the same as the pyramids in Egypt.

Agnes asked me if I would allow myself to be led to a power centre on the land so we headed towards a stream running through the lush green landscape.

I found two huge rocks that called out for me to sit on.

I gravitated towards the larger of the two and Agnes said it was the male of the two.

She then sat next to me and handed me a small woven bag decorated in feathers. She said it was a gift for responding to her request of the drawing and the energy work I do for the planet and people.

I slowly looked inside the bag to find a massive piece of greenstone. It was a mere and in the Maori culture, was used during communications. It was known that if you were holding one of them, you would be speaking the truth. It was beautiful and I was completely lost for words.

"His name is Nga hau e wha, which means the Essence or Breath of the Four Winds"

The name was applicable as we were sitting within the temple of the Four Winds.

"And along with this I have been told to pass on a Maori name for you. It is 'Ki Wahine ko hikoi Te Whenua', which means The Woman Who Walks the Earth."

Agnes and Daphnie asked that I lead them from this point on, as this trip was important for me.

Feeling honoured I felt as though we needed to take a drive up into the mountains.

On the way up it was explained to me that the two mountains I was being drawn to were male and female.

I directed John Boy to as close to the middle of them as possible. The road in fact took us right up onto the ridge between the two mountains and at the top was a large tree. I had to get out of the car and stand under it.

The energy pouring through the tree was incredible but there was also an intense sadness.

Agnes and Daphnie then joined me and we went in to a meditation.

Instantly I was taken deep into the earth and felt a huge blockage. As I moved closer to the block I felt streams of emotion and the sense of it being connected to the September 11 bombings.

Light then began pouring through me as it streamed into the blockage. All the emotions connected to this event rushed through the earth between the trees as the blockage was released.

I stood for ten minutes as the pain and suffering continued to flow. As the energy point became clearer and the last of the emotions had passed through the portal I was shown a vision of New Zealand being a powerful place on the planet.

All energies coming into the planet have to be filtered through this land and all energies being released from the planet also have to pass though this land. I felt honoured to be a part of this special land.

It had been a long day and all of us were hungry and tired so we headed back to John Boys for the night.

After a wonderful meal we sat and talked for hours. I eventually couldn't stay awake anymore and headed off to get at least a couple of hours sleep. I began drifting off to sleep as soon as my head hit the pillow but before I could totally succumb I was greeted by the presence of a Maori Chief in spirit.

With a full-face moko he was carrying a taiaha, which he handed to me as he said "Te Owanga Te Papa Iwi."

I had no idea what that meant but I knew he was handing me a responsibility and title he had carried until that point.

I felt the burden and honour that came with it, and knew that somehow it was to do with the Maori, Native American and Egyptian peoples.

Sleep enveloped me and I could feel it was going to be an intense sleep.

I talked to Agnes the next day about what I received and she agreed that I was being handed an important purpose.

As we were talking I suddenly remembered that I had actually seen the Maori Chief before.

On one of the occasions we went down country for our holidays when I was a child, Helen and I were swimming in the river when a Maori Chief appeared on the river bank. He was dressed in a cape and was holding the taiaha I had just seen again.

Helen had run screaming from the river but I stayed and watched him with a sense of calm and familiarity.

It was a strange feeling to know that he had probably been close to me most of my life.

I also remembered that on the same trip I used to wander up in to the hills by myself.

Once there, I would play with a girl with very white skin and long blonde hair.

I remember the feeling surrounding the experience to be ethereal and I had learnt recently that she was in fact a patupaiarehe or Fairy person.

I was always aware of others watching on as we played, danced and sang and on one occasion on my journey back to the school house I became stuck in sinking sand. There were several of them that appeared and pulled me out and I recalled how they had placed some energy over me so I wouldn't remember.

Despite not being Maori I had a deep connection with them and the Native American Indians.

I felt blessed to have had these experiences in my life and was excited about working with the ancient people of the lands in a whole new way.

I realised my life was about to change again and I would have to prepare for my next big journey..

ABOUT THE AUTHOR

Leigh currently lives back in her homeland of New Zealand where she lives with her daughter and animals.
She continues healing work with both land and people and has developed a natural skin care range as well as creating Orgonite.
Art is still an important part of her life and can be found at: www.nativeimpressionsart.com
Her second book – 'The South American Connection' will be available from 2016.
All correspondence can be made through info@theonenesssanctuary.info

www.ingramcontent.com/pod-product-compliance
Lightning Source LLC
Chambersburg PA
CBHW031958050726
47590CB00006B/1957